Praise for *Making Better Decisions*

"The book is a modern take on decision making. The innovative scope will inspire instructors by encouraging them to include a combination rather than a subset of decision-theoretic, statistical, behavioral, and philosophical concepts in their courses."

Marzena J. Rostek, University of Wisconsin

"Written by a leading authority and teacher in the area of decision theory, this is a terrific combined textbook–handbook for students and practitioners of management. Indeed, it is a terrific book for everyone interested in 'making better decisions.'"

Adam Brandenburger, New York University

"This book is extremely effective for anyone who wants to acquire quick, basic understanding of old and new concepts of decision theory, with a minimum level of technical details."

Ehud Kalai, Northwestern University

To Eva, Alma, and Erga

Making Better Decisions
Decision Theory in Practice

Itzhak Gilboa

A John Wiley & Sons, Ltd., Publication

This edition first published 2011
© 2011 John Wiley & Sons, Inc.

Blackwell Publishing was acquired by John Wiley & Sons in February 2007. Blackwell's publishing program has been merged with Wiley's global Scientific, Technical, and Medical business to form Wiley-Blackwell.

Registered Office
John Wiley & Sons Ltd, The Atrium, Southern Gate, Chichester, West Sussex, PO19 8SQ, United Kingdom

Editorial Offices
350 Main Street, Malden, MA 02148-5020, USA
9600 Garsington Road, Oxford, OX4 2DQ, UK
The Atrium, Southern Gate, Chichester, West Sussex, PO19 8SQ, UK

For details of our global editorial offices, for customer services, and for information about how to apply for permission to reuse the copyright material in this book please see our web site at www.wiley.com/wiley-blackwell.

Library of Congress Cataloging-in-Publication Data

Gilboa, Itzhak.
Making better decisions : decision theory in practice / Itzhak Gilboa.
   p. cm.
Includes bibliographical references and index.
   ISBN 978-1-4443-3651-1 (hardback) – ISBN 978-1-4443-3652-8 (pbk. : alk. paper)
1. Decision making. I. Title.
   QA279.4.G554 2011
   658.4′03–dc22

A catalogue record for this book is available from the British Library.

Set in 10.5/13.5pt Palatino by SPi Publisher Services, Pondicherry, India.
Printed in Singapore by Ho Printing Singapore Pte Ltd

02 2011

Contents

Contents

Preface

This book can be used as a textbook for a course in management or economics. It can also be used as a self-help book for interested readers. The material is presented in a very informal and non-mathematical form, and the book does not get into the nuts and bolts of the theory. Readers who are convinced that they could make better decisions by applying decision theory seriously may well need to use more technical textbooks and/or the advice of experts. The goal of this book is to generate awareness of potential problems as well as possible solutions.

A word to teachers: I recommend asking the students to cope with the problems at the beginning of each chapter on their own. In two out of the five chapters the problems appear in two versions, titled "Group A" and "Group B." Mostly, the problems of the two groups are slightly different, and the comparison between the answers to similar problems is the heart of the matter. If possible, students might be divided into two groups, get only their questionnaire, and cope with the problems on their own before class discussion. The book's web site (www.wiley.com/go/gilboa) has a downloadable file with the questionnaires, so that these can be distributed before the students get to read the book. It is also possible to have students work on the problems in class. In any event, it is important that each student works on only one version of each problem. If time allows, students can also work in class in small groups, and compare the answers they come up with individually with the answers they choose after a group discussion. The book's web site also has PowerPoint slides that you may use in class.

A word to out-of-class readers: It is recommended that you think about the problems in the order they are presented, and try to imagine what your answer would be if you were solving either only the first or only the second questionnaire. You may also take a break of a day or two between the two questionnaires.

Whether the book is used as a textbook or a self-help book, the juxtaposition of problems is not designed to make anyone feel bad about "not getting it right." The goal is only to illustrate certain points in a clear and memorable way.

Acknowledgments

I am grateful to my teachers, colleagues, and friends who have greatly influenced my thinking about decision making over the years. I cannot possibly thank all these researchers and friends, but I would be amiss not to mention David Schmeidler, who was my graduate advisor and has remained a close friend and collaborator ever since; Edi Karni, who taught me my first course on decision theory; and Peter Wakker, who, since our days as graduate students, has been and remains a wonderful source of knowledge on theory, experiments, and applications. I have benefited no less from the numerous students whom I have taught over the years. Without their input, inquisitive questions, and class discussions, I would not have understood how the theory relates to actual decisions.

I also wish to thank Valerie Gauthier of HEC, Paris, for her encouragement, and the reviewers and editors who commented on earlier drafts of this book. Finally, I thank Carmel Israeli for bibliographical help.

1

Background

This book is designed to acquaint you with some ideas from decision theory, and to examine how they might help in making better decisions. The method of presentation is based on problems in which you are asked to imagine a situation, and make a decision or a judgment. The problems are chosen to exemplify some principles of decision theory, as well as violations of these principles derived from the psychological literature.

What are "better decisions" and who has the authority to judge what a good decision is? The answers are not obvious. I take the view that the quality of a decision is, in the final analysis, a judgment to be made by the decision maker. That is, a "good," or a "better," decision should be so judged by the one who makes it. Decision makers may need to be exposed to some analysis and reasoning about their decisions; they may also need some experience to be able to judge their decisions with the appropriate perspective. But eventually, it is the decision makers themselves who should feel that they make better decisions. If decision theorists preach a certain mode of decision making, but they do not manage to convince decision makers that this mode is "right," then it probably isn't.

Making Better Decisions, by Itzhak Gilboa © 2011 John Wiley & Sons, Inc.

Borrowing an economic metaphor, I view people like me – namely, decision theorists – as merchants. We buy decision principles (mostly from the forefathers of decision theory) and try to sell them to decision makers. These are our consumers, and the consumers should feel they are happy with the product they have bought. This doesn't mean that all consumers should be happy at all stages of the process. Sometimes acquiring knowledge might take some patience. It's also possible that some people will find parts of this book useful but not others. But if most readers find most of the book useless, there's something wrong with the product I'm selling.

I usually start with examples in which classical decision theory is violated. Many such examples were provided by the psychologists Daniel Kahneman and Amos Tversky.[1] They and their followers ran carefully designed laboratory experiments which showed that almost all rationality assumptions in economics may be violated, in certain examples, by a non-negligible portion of decision makers.[2] Other examples predate the works of Kahneman and Tversky. In any event, it should be emphasized that for practically every general principle there will be examples in which it will be violated by many decision makers.[3]

I believe that the best way to explain a principle is to start with an example that violates it. In general, it is useful to understand a theory by that which it rules out, and a few good examples are the best way to envision the general principle. Moreover, in the case of decision making, observing a violation of a certain theory, or principle, also raises a question that each of us has to cope with on her or his own: do I like to be the kind of decision maker who violates this principle and, if so, when, and under what conditions? Seeing an example in which I violated a certain principle, and then understanding what the principle suggests, I can next judge whether I wish to change my behavior in the future or not.

In a sense, you may consider this book as a catalog of patterns of decision making that some theorists consider to be irrational. I use these patterns both to present the general principles, but also to criticize them. As explained above, I will try not to offer a supposedly correct answer as to which principles we should adopt and when.

This decision should be made by each and every decision maker. I believe that, whatever is your answer, you will be enriched by understanding the general principles and by being acquainted with examples in which these principles tend to be violated.

It might be useful to mention two terms that decision theorists and economists like to use in this context: descriptive and normative theories. A *descriptive* theory is meant to describe reality. For instance, the claim that demand curves slope down attempts to tell us something about the world. Importantly, it does not make a value judgment and takes no stand on whether this feature of the world is good or bad.

A *normative* theory is a recommendation to decision makers, a suggestion regarding how they *should* make decisions. For instance, the claim that we should reduce income inequality is a normative claim. Note that the word "normative" does not mean here "the norm in a given society" as it does in other social sciences. The term only says something about the type of interaction between the theorist and the decision maker, namely, that this is an instance in which the former is trying to convince the latter to behave in a certain way.

In decision theory it is often the case that a principle can be interpreted either descriptively or normatively. Consider the theory that each economic agent maximizes a utility function. I may propose it as descriptive, namely, arguing that this is a good description of real economic agents. And I may promote it as normative, in which case my claim will be that you would be wise to become such an agent. As a descriptive theory, the principle is tested for its correspondence to reality. The better it fits the data, the more successful it is. As a normative one, the principle should not fit reality. In fact, there is no point in giving decision makers recommendations that they anyway follow. Rather, the test is whether the decision makers *would like* to follow the principle.

It is important to realize that you will typically be interested in both normative and descriptive theories. A good normative theory is one that you would like to adopt, that is, one that would allow you to make better decisions in your own eyes. A good descriptive theory will tell you how people around you behave. Whether you interact with your boss or your underlings, colleagues or customers, competitors or other traders, it is important to know how they make decisions.

There is a delicate point here. When we teach the foundations of microeconomics, for example, we typically assume that agents are rational. If this happens to be a good descriptive theory, you may use it to make better decisions in the market, and this seems like fair play. But when we focus on modes of behavior that are considered irrational (at least by some), an ethical issue emerges. Suppose that we are convinced that a certain mode of behavior is silly, and that we would like to avoid it. It so happens that many people are not aware of our analysis and they still follow it. Knowing this fact might be useful, but is it morally right? Will we be justified in making better decisions for ourselves, relying, as it were, on other people's mistakes? And if not, will not a book such as this make the world a worse place, helping some decision makers take advantage of others?

These are serious concerns. Nevertheless, I do not hesitate to teach the material presented here or to publish this book. There are two main reasons for this. First, I do not believe that such knowledge can be kept confidential. Too many people know of this material (including the work of Kahneman and Tversky) for this to be a secret. Second, many if not most practitioners who could benefit from this knowledge had already done so years before it made its way into the realm of academic knowledge. Many of the effects that Kahneman and Tversky documented in their careful studies had been made use of by marketing people and politicians, among others. Hence, one might hope that such a book will do more good than harm, because it will help the unprofessional make better decisions in the presence of the professionals.

Notes

1 Daniel Kahneman received the Nobel Prize in Economics in 2002 for his contributions in this area. Amos Tversky died in 1996.

2   See, for instance, Kahneman, D., Slovic, P. and Tversky, A. (eds) (1982) *Judgment under Uncertainty: Heuristics and Biases*. Cambridge University Press.

3   Amos Tversky used to say: "Give me an axiom, and I'll design the experiment that refutes it."

Suggested Reading

On the foundations of theories of rational choice:

Binmore, K. (2009) *Rational Decisions*. Princeton University Press.

Gilboa, I. (2010) *Rational Choice*. MIT Press.

Hammond, J. S., Keeney, R. and Raiffa, H. (1998) *Smart Choices: A Practical Guide to Making Better Decisions*. Harvard Business School Press.

On the psychology of choice and violations of classical theories:

Ariely, D. (2008) *Predictably Irrational*. MIT Press.

Bazerman, M. H. and Moore, D. (2006) *Judgment in Managerial Decision Making*. John Wiley & Sons, Inc.

Thaler, R. H. and Sunstein, C. R. (2008) *Nudge: Improving Decisions About Health, Wealth, and Happiness*. Yale University Press.

2

Judgment and Choice Biases

Introduction

This chapter discusses a variety of examples in which people tend to make judgments or decisions that are considered to be "biases" or "mistakes," at least by some. Many of these examples contradict the classical theories of rational choice used in economics and related fields. Some violate explicit assumptions of economic theory. Others violate implicit assumptions and often cannot even be discussed in the language of economics.

Most of these examples were suggested and tested experimentally by Daniel Kahneman and Amos Tversky and their followers. Kahneman and Tversky started their project in the late 1960s. For many years researchers in various fields did not take their findings as much more than amusing examples for cocktail party chat. Economists dismissed the examples on the grounds that many of the experiments did not involve monetary payoffs, arguing that people's behavior would be much closer to classical economic predictions if significant amounts were at stake. Often an evolutionary argument was also quoted: if such silly and suboptimal behavior exists, there will be agents in the market who will take advantage of it, and it will be driven out by the

Making Better Decisions, by Itzhak Gilboa © 2011 John Wiley & Sons, Inc.

evolutionary forces of the market. Finally, there was a claim that many of the examples are artificial and contrived, and do not represent the typical behavior of real agents in naturally occurring situations.

Over the years things have changed. In the 1990s researchers in economics and finance started expanding the scope of their models to encompass some types of behavior that were found in experimental studies though they were at odds with the classical theory. The fields of behavioral economics and behavioral finance flourished, and the 2002 Nobel Prize in Economics, awarded to Daniel Kahneman, recognized the impact of psychological research on economics. However, this recognition did not settle the debate, and the importance and validity of psychological experiments for economics are still topics of heated controversy.

The main goal of this book is to help you make better decisions for yourself, that is, to change your decision making procedures so that you will like your decisions better. For this normative purpose, the controversy mentioned above is not very relevant. We will go over examples in which some people behave in ways that they find silly, and you will be urged to ask yourself whether you sometimes make such decisions and whether you think that they can be improved upon. You may find that you are a textbook *Homo economicus* who never behaves in a way that anyone considers suboptimal. Alternatively, you may find that you sometimes deviate from this model, but that you actually like the way you make decisions even when you do. In both cases you will not gain much from the exercise, though no harm will be done either. However, if you find some cases in which you make decisions that you don't like, and decide to adopt a procedure that can help you avoid such decisions in the future, you will have gained something. The examples presented here were selected with these scenarios in mind. They are designed to help you think about your own decisions, and whether they are natural or contrived, typical or rare, they serve their purpose.

If, however, you wish to use the examples for descriptive purposes, that is, to understand and predict how people around you behave, a few words of warning are in order. First, the argument that some examples are extreme, contrived, or artificial has been made also within psychology.[1] In fact, there is an ongoing debate about the degree to which the violations of rational theories are typical in naturally occurring decision situations. Some findings suggest that people tend to make decisions better in tasks and contexts that are familiar to them than in unfamiliar ones.[2] Thus, if one were hoping to exploit other people's biases and mistakes, one would be well advised to take into account the possibility that these biases might be less prevalent in real life than in classroom experiments. It is possible to benefit from other people's suboptimal behavior, but the present collection of examples is not designed for this purpose.

Second, knowledge in the social sciences is typically qualified and limited. We know of very few general laws that can be thought of as universal or eternal as are the laws of the natural sciences. Social and economic systems are very complex, and they keep changing, sometimes as a result of research about them. Consequently, my advice is to take any scientific finding about the behavior of people, economies, or societies with a spoonful of salt. It is not a priori clear that the lessons learnt from one group of agents generalize to another. Real-estate agents in California need not have the same decision modes as cereal consumers in Belgium. In psychology it is well accepted that empirical knowledge does not automatically generalize from one group to another, and that experiments need to be replicated. Sometimes a finding that is true of adults does not hold for adolescents, and a phenomenon that was found in women does not generalize to men. Similarly, any particular violation of classical choice theory that we discuss here may be more prevalent in some groups of agents and less in others, and it is even possible that some of them are less prevalent today than they were 30 years ago.

To conclude, you may view the following pages as raising questions about decision making. The answers, describing how people actually make decisions, have to be constantly updated and adapted. The questions, by contrast, are timeless.

Most of the material in this chapter can be understood without any prior knowledge. However, if you have never taken any class in microeconomic theory, and you feel that *Homo economicus* is a complete stranger to you, Appendix A provides a little background.

Problems – Group A

Problem 2.1

A 65-year-old relative of yours suffers from a serious disease. It makes her life miserable, but does not pose an immediate risk to her life. She can go through an operation that, if successful, will cure her. However, the operation is risky; 30% of the patients undergoing it die. Would you recommend that she undergoes it?

Problem 2.2

You are given $1,000 for sure. Which of the following two options would you prefer?
a. To get an additional $500 for sure.
b. To get another $1,000 with probability 50%, and otherwise nothing (and be left with the first $1,000).

Problem 2.3

You go to a movie. It was supposed to be good, but it turns out to be boring. Would you leave in the middle and do something else instead?

Problem 2.4

Linda is 31 years old, single, outspoken, and very bright. She majored in philosophy. As a student, she was deeply concerned with issues of discrimination and social justice, and she participated in anti-nuclear demonstrations.

Rank order the following eight descriptions in terms of the probability (likelihood) that they describe Linda:

a. Linda is a teacher in an elementary school.
b. Linda works in a bookstore and takes yoga classes.
c. Linda is active in a feminist movement.
d. Linda is a psychiatric social worker.
e. Linda is a member of the League of Women Voters.
f. Linda is a bank teller.
g. Linda is an insurance salesperson.
h. Linda is a bank teller who is active in a feminist movement.

Problem 2.5

In four pages of a novel (about 2,000 words) in English, do you expect to find more than 10 words that have the form $\_\_\_\_\_n\_$ (seven-letter words that have the letter n in the sixth position)?

Problem 2.6

What is the probability that, in the next two years, there will be a cure for AIDS?

Problem 2.7

What is the probability that, during the next year, your car could be a "total loss" due to an accident?

Problem 2.8

Which of the following causes more deaths?
a. Digestive diseases.
b. Motor vehicle accidents.

_____

_____

Problem 2.9

A newly hired engineer for a computer firm in Melbourne, Australia, has four years of experience and good all-round qualifications.

   Do you think that her annual salary is above or below $65,000?

_____

_____

   What is your estimate of her salary?

_____

_____

Problem 2.10

You have bought a ticket to a concert, which cost you $50. When you arrive at the concert hall, you find you have lost the ticket. Would you buy another one (assuming you have enough money in your wallet)?

_____

_____

Problem 2.11

Which of the following two options do you prefer?

a. Receiving $10 today.
b. Receiving $12 a week from today.

Problems – Group B

Problem 2.12

A 65-year-old relative of yours suffers from a serious disease. It makes her life miserable, but does not pose an immediate risk to her life. She can go through an operation that, if successful, will cure her. However, the operation is risky; 70% of the patients undergoing it survive. Would you recommend that she undergoes it?

Problem 2.13

You are given $2,000 for sure. Which of the following two options would you prefer?
a. To lose $500 for sure.
b. To lose $1,000 with probability 50%, and otherwise to lose nothing.

Problem 2.14

Your friend had a ticket to a movie. She couldn't make it, and gave you the ticket "instead of just throwing it away." The movie was supposed to be good, but it turns out to be boring. Would you leave in the middle and do something else instead?

_____

_____

Problem 2.15

Linda is 31 years old, single, outspoken, and very bright. She majored in philosophy. As a student, she was deeply concerned with issues of discrimination and social justice, and she participated in anti-nuclear demonstrations.

    Rank order the following eight descriptions in terms of the probability (likelihood) that they describe Linda:

a. Linda is a teacher in an elementary school.
b. Linda works in a bookstore and takes yoga classes.
c. Linda is active in a feminist movement.
d. Linda is a psychiatric social worker.
e. Linda is a member of the League of Women Voters.
f. Linda is a bank teller.
g. Linda is an insurance salesperson.
h. Linda is a bank teller who is active in a feminist movement.

_____

_____

Problem 2.16

In four pages of a novel (about 2,000 words) in English, do you expect to find more than 10 words that have the form _ _ _ _ *ing* (seven-letter words that end with *ing*)?

_____

_____

13

Problem 2.17

What is the probability that, in the next two years, there will be a new genetic discovery in the study of apes, and a cure for AIDS?

_____

_____

Problem 2.18

What is the probability that, during the next year, your car could be a "total loss" due to:
a. An accident in which the other driver is drunk?
b. An accident for which you are responsible?
c. An accident occurring while your car is parked on the street?
d. An accident occurring while your car is parked in a garage?
e. One of the above?

_____

_____

Problem 2.19

Which of the following causes more deaths?
a. Digestive diseases.
b. Motor vehicle accidents.

_____

_____

Problem 2.20

A newly hired engineer for a computer firm in Melbourne, Australia, has four years of experience and good all-round qualifications.

Do you think that her annual salary is above or below $135,000?

What is your estimate of her salary?

Problem 2.21

You are going to a concert. Tickets cost $50. When you arrive at the concert hall, you find you have lost a $50 bill. Would you still buy the ticket (assuming you have enough money in your wallet)?

Problem 2.22

Which of the following two options do you prefer?
a. Receiving $10 fifty weeks from today.
b. Receiving $12 fifty-one weeks from today.

Framing Effects

Consider Problems 2.1 and 2.12. Their text is very similar:

A 65-year-old relative of yours suffers from a serious disease. It makes her life miserable, but does not pose an immediate risk to her life. She can go through an operation that, if successful, will cure her.

> However, the operation is risky; [Problem 2.1: 30% of the patients undergoing it die. Problem 2.12: 70% of the patients undergoing it survive]. Would you recommend that she undergoes it?

These two problems are identical. The only difference in the text is that one of them gives the information in terms of probability of death, and the other in terms of probability of survival. But it is the same information. It doesn't take more than a moment's reflection to realize that, if 30% of the patients die, then 70% of them survive, and vice versa. In other words, the two problems only differ in the representation of the information provided.

Yet, people often make different decisions in the two problems above. If you consider two large groups of randomly selected decision makers, and you give each group one of these problems, you are likely to find that a larger percentage of people recommend undergoing the operation in Problem 2.12 than in Problem 2.1. This is a variant of a famous example used by Kahneman and Tversky to exemplify the *framing effect*: the effect that the frame, or the representation, has on the decision.[3]

The mechanism of the framing effect is not hard to imagine, once the phenomenon is pointed out to you: different representations of the same information can induce different associations in our minds. These can change our emotional reaction as well as our assessment of probabilities. It is natural that I don't like risking my life. Given the choice between two options, one that involves risk of death and another that doesn't, it makes sense that I would need particularly good reasons to choose the former over the latter. As a result, there is an almost automatic reaction away from choices that may risk my life, and the very word "death" is a signal that an option is of this type. Hence, when I hear the word "death," a red light inside my mind starts blinking "danger," and I am more likely to try to avoid the option associated with death. By contrast, when I hear the word "survival," it connotes positive thoughts and emotions. Thus, a decision that is explicitly related to survival is more attractive than one that is explicitly related to death.

The difficulty is that, typically, a decision that *may* result in survival may also result in death and vice versa. When I present the problem to you, I can choose to highlight one or the other, but both possibilities exist irrespective of the representation I choose. This is why most people feel that it is irrational to make different decisions in the two problems above. Let me remind you that according to the rules of the game we play, it is up to you to determine what is rational *for you*. Thus, if you insist that you're OK with making different decisions in the two problems, then it is rational for you to do so and that's that. However, I have tried this example in many classes, and I have yet to find a student who insists that this is rational. This does not mean, of course, that no one makes different decisions in the two problems: framing effects do work, and people do tend to make different decisions. But they do not seem to like that. When people are tricked by this example, they are not very proud of their decision. Hence, it is irrational for them to make different decisions in different framings of the same problem.

Next consider Problems 2.2 and 2.13. The former reads:

You are given $1,000 for sure. Which of the following two options would you prefer?

a. To get an additional $500 for sure.
b. To get another $1,000 with probability 50%, and otherwise nothing (and be left with the first $1,000).

Whereas Problem 2.13 reads:

You are given $2,000 for sure. Which of the following two options would you prefer?

a. To lose $500 for sure.
b. To lose $1,000 with probability 50%, and otherwise to lose nothing.

Here, again, we have two different representations of the same alternatives. Observe that we are asked to make a choice before we are given anything. Thus, whether we first get $1,000 and then additional money ($500 for sure or another $1,000 with probability 50%) or first get $2,000 and then lose some money ($500 for sure or $1,000 with probability 50%) should make no difference. Put differently, if you ignore the words "get" and "lose" in the second stage, the choice in *both* problems is between

a. Getting $1,500 for sure.
b. Getting $1,000 with probability 50%, and $2,000 with probability 50%.

The two problems above are simply different representations of this problem. Hence, most people tend to feel that they would have liked to make the same decision in Problems 2.2 and 2.13. Again, the claim is not that most people *do* make the same decision in the two problems. It is, rather, that most people *would like* to make the same decision. In other words, if you consider the theoretical claim that "people are not affected by the representation of alternatives," the existence of framing effects has to do with its descriptive validity: the more prevalent are framing effects, the less accurate is this theory as a description of reality. However, the theory can still be a good normative theory: if people accept it as a desirable goal, and if, furthermore, they find it irrational not to follow it, then this theory can be a useful guide in their decision making.

The equivalence of the two representations in Problems 2.2 and 2.13 is not always accepted as universally as the equivalence between Problems 2.1 and 2.12. Some people feel that losing money that they already had is very different from getting money that they never had, even if the bottom line is the same. Indeed, this has to do with other phenomena found by Kahneman and Tversky and Richard Thaler, known as "loss aversion" and "endowment effect," to be discussed later. These phenomena are important and well established. Moreover, we will discuss situations in which you may find them rational. For example, if you have become used to having a certain amount of wealth, giving it up may be quite different from not having it in the first place. But in the present case we are discussing money that is promised to you, but that you have not yet received. You didn't even have enough time to get used to the idea that this money will be yours, to start planning what you'll do with it, and so on. Rather, you're told that you will get some money, and you immediately keep reading the relevant choices. Hence many people are convinced that their choices in Problems 2.2 and 2.13 should be the same. But, again, it is your decision whether it is irrational to have your choice depend on the representation of the outcomes in this case.

Examples of framing effects abound. In the United States, gas stations often have two posted prices – the "regular" one, which applies to credit card purchases, and a "cash discount" price, applying only to cash purchases. It's easy to understand why the two prices might differ. But why don't we observe the cash price as being the default and the higher one as a "credit surcharge" price? Clearly, the practical implications would be the same – you pay one price with credit card and another, lower price when you use cash. However, representation matters. Suppose that I need gas, drive by the station, but find that I have no cash in my wallet. I can easily tell myself, "OK, I'll pay the regular price – I'm not the kind of guy who has to get the discount whenever possible," and buy gas. By contrast, if the cash price were perceived as the "regular" (default) price, and there were a credit surcharge, I might have reacted by saying, "That's really unfair! Do I need to pay a fine for using my card? Are they trying to exploit the fact that I forgot to withdraw cash?" – and I might decide to look for another gas station, one that treats its customers more fairly. Thus, the representation of the same menu of prices can result in different behavior.

Next consider a politician running for office, say, the presidency. Suppose that he says, "I intend to make health costs tax deductible." This sounds like a social policy that favors people with difficulties: if someone is sick and has a hard time financing health care that is not provided by the state, the state would help them out by deducting these costs from their pre-tax income. Assume now that the same candidate says, "I would like to have the state subsidize health costs. And I will give a higher percentage subsidy to the rich than to the poor." Clearly, this doesn't sound great. Why would the rich get a higher percentage subsidy than the poor? However, this policy means precisely the same thing as the previous one. Making a certain expense tax deductible is tantamount to subsidizing it, where the rate of subsidy is the marginal tax rate. Richer people, who are typically paying a higher marginal tax rate, will enjoy a greater deduction than poor people. To consider an extreme case, a person who has no income and therefore pays no taxes will not benefit from a tax deduction at all.

These two examples suggest that framing effects are quite common. Indeed, we'd expect marketing people as well as politicians to be masterful at "framing" options in attractive ways. People whose job it is to try to sell something to us typically have a good feel as to which representations work better than others.

Brainstorming and Formal Models

What can be done to avoid framing effects? More generally, how can we avoid mistakes, that is, decisions or evaluations that we might consider silly?

First, awareness is key. Being aware of various types of biases, mistakes, and psychological effects is an important step in trying to identify them in our reasoning or decision making processes, and in attempting to avoid them. Second, the use of formal models may be of great help. Finally, working in groups and brainstorming often helps. This should be qualified, because group decisions are not always better than individual decisions. Groups that differ in their motivation may find it hard to make coherent decisions, and if they do, the decisions may be very conservative, and may also be swayed by charismatic personalities. But individuals who discuss a problem together and then go their own ways to make individual decisions will generally make better decisions than they would on their own. Groups do tend to be better than individuals in sheer analysis,[4] with many ideas being brought up, challenged by others, compared, and analyzed.

In the case of framing effects, formal models are often all that is needed. In fact, we can even use them as a definition of "framing effects": these are the effects that disappear when a formal model is introduced. For example, if, in Problem 2.1, you were to write down the choices in a formal model, you'd represent undergoing the operation as a distribution over outcomes. Such creatures are lists of probability numbers that need to sum up to 1. Hence, if there is 30% probability of death, you'll have to write down also the complement event, namely, survival, and find that it has a probability of 70%. And if you were to start with Problem 2.12, by similar reasoning you would end up with the same distribution. In other words, if you put upon yourself the discipline of using formal models, you won't be able to attach importance to the representation, and you will be immune to the framing effect.

The same logic applies to Problems 2.2 and 2.13. If you write down a formal model, you need to represent the choices as distributions over outcomes. It may take you a few seconds to do it, but at the end you'll see that the choice is between a gain of $1,500 for sure and a gain of $1,000 or $2,000 with equal probabilities. Similarly, in the gas station example a formal model would be a list of payment methods and corresponding prices, where words such as "discount" and "surcharge" have no room. Finally, the tax deduction example is one in which people pay different amounts depending on their income and their health costs. If you write down a table (or a function) describing the amount of money a person is left with given these two inputs, you'll find that the two representations describe the same table.[5]

In short, formal models may be of great help in making better decisions, even though we should not expect the formal model to give us the "correct" answer. It is very seldom the case that there is a correct answer that can be calculated in a mathematical model. These cases are, in a sense, less interesting, because you can relegate the computation of the "correct answer" to a piece of software or a consultant. Most of our problems, however, are not of this type. Typically, answers depend on subjective judgments, opinions, and values. But our thinking about these problems can be greatly simplified and clarified by the use of formal models. Framing effects are an extreme example in which the use of a formal model helps you avoid the psychological bias, without restricting your actual choices in any way.

It is important to distinguish between formal models and mathematical sophistication. Using a formal, mathematical model does not necessarily mean that you solve complicated equations, or that you expect the right choice to emerge out of a calculation that normal people can barely follow. In fact, there is a danger of over-mathematization that you should be aware of: often experts focus on those parts of the problem that are amenable to mathematical analysis, and discard those that are hard to measure or specify. And when decision makers find it difficult to follow the mathematical reasoning, they sometimes accept the conclusions without questioning the assumptions. This is not the type of formal modeling that I try to promote here. Rather, I suggest using the language of mathematics as a way to abstract away from details of the problem, without discarding anything of importance. Therefore, the formal model will often not have a clear-cut answer, because it will have too many unspecified parameters. But the very exercise of thinking in terms of a formal model will greatly help you sharpen your intuition, and should not result in worse decisions.

In the following we will see many other psychological biases, and most of them will not disappear as soon as a formal model is used. Some of these formal models will also suggest that certain choices are better, or more coherent, than others. But it is important to bear in mind that the use of formal models is not a substitute for further analysis or for group brainstorming.

Endowment Effect

As mentioned above, different choices in Problems 2.2 and 2.13 can also be explained by the *endowment effect*, attributed to Richard Thaler.[6] It is defined as the tendency to value what we have more than what we do not yet have. In the example above, $1,000 that I already have will be "worth" more to me than the same amount I do not yet have. Hence, it is easier for me to risk not getting this amount if I do not think it's mine, than to lose it if I think it is. (We will go back to the asymmetry between gains and losses, and to loss aversion, later on.)

The endowment effect is not mainly about money. It can be viewed as a manifestation of a general principle called the *status quo bias*,[7] and, in the context of economic trade, it can manifest itself with respect to various goods. Consider the following experiment. We are trying to find out the value of a coffee mug for students. (This experiment was run with college students.[8] Researchers often find that the easiest way to get participants for experiments is to sample students in their universities. Psychologists are aware of the fact that not all findings from college students will generalize to the rest of the population.) Here are three different ways to try to assess it:

1. Ask the students how much they are willing to pay in order to get the mug.
2. Tell the students that each of them is going to get a gift. It can be either the mug or a sum of money. Ask them what amount of money would make them indifferent between the mug and the money.
3. Give each student the mug as a gift. (You may also let them use it once, to really make them feel it's theirs.) Now ask them how much we will need to pay them in order to buy the mug from them.

It seems like all three answers should be similar. But even according to economic theory, the answers need not be identical, because in the first condition the students do not get any gifts, and in the last two they do. More precisely, assume that a student's "bundle" is a pair (m, n), where m is the amount of money the student has, and n is the number of coffee mugs in their possession. Let us say that a student starts off with $(m, 0)$, that is, a certain amount of money m and no coffee mugs. Question (1) looks for a price p such that

$$(m-p, 1) \sim (m, 0)$$

That is, we ask what price p would make the student indifferent between giving up the amount of money p, being left with $m - p$, and getting the mug, versus not giving up any money and not getting the mug.

Question (2), by contrast, asks what the amount of money q is such that getting q as a gift (resulting in $m + q$ dollars but no mugs) would be equivalent to getting a mug (but no money). That is, which q solves the "preference equation"

$$(m + q, 0) \sim (m, 1)$$

Finally, consider question (3). Here the student gets the mug as a gift, and therefore has a bundle $(m, 1)$. Now we ask them how much we should pay to buy the mug from them. That is, by how much should we increase their amount of money m so that they'd be willing to go down from 1 mug to 0 mugs. This translates to asking which q solves

$$(m + q, 0) \sim (m, 1)$$

Clearly, economic theory predicts that the answers to (2) and (3) will be identical. The answer to (1) may differ. For example, p cannot exceed m, while q can. Indeed, if I were offering you the rent of a very nice apartment rather than a coffee mug, you may have a very high q (getting the use of the apartment as a gift) while you may not be able to afford to pay so much out of your existing income m.

The interesting finding was that the answers in (3) were much higher than the answers in (2) and (1), with (2) being above (1). The average answers were \$2.87 for (1), \$3.12 for (2), and \$7.12 for (3). That is, the biggest difference in the answers occurred precisely where economic theory would have predicted no difference at all.

Why do we observe the endowment effect and is it rational? There are several reasons why it may make a lot of sense to exhibit the endowment effect, and more generally the status quo bias. These reasons may also explain why we evolved to have these biases. Among the reasons are:

a. *Information:* When we own something, we know it better than when we don't. There may not be much to know about a coffee mug, but if you think of a computer or a car, you realize that there may be various problems with the unknown product.

Having owned and consumed a product, you know its quality. Thus, a new product is actually a lottery, an uncertain choice, as far as your utility is concerned. If you don't like risk, you will prefer the product that you already know.

b. *Transaction costs:* If we had no status quo bias, we would be switching between different choices much more often than we do. Consider the following example. Your child comes home and says that he wants to study math. After one year he's back saying that math has no future, and that he really wants to study physics. A year later, and it's law. Later still he finds that economics is the thing for him. At some point you're likely to say, "Hey, why don't you choose something and finish it, to have *some* degree?" The point is that at every stage your child might be right in the assessment that an alternative choice is better than the one he's made. But information is noisy and what looks good today may not look so great tomorrow. If every time a certain alternative looks better than what we have, perhaps even only a little bit better, we switch to it, we may never get anywhere. By contrast, a preference for the status quo adds stability to our choices. It prevents us making too frequent changes, which have their own cost.

c. *Habit formation:* We get used to certain products. Sometimes it's a matter of changing tastes: you can get used to a particular brand of cereal, or beer, to an extent that your taste buds truly demand this product and no other. Sometimes it's a matter of routine: you may not have a strong preference between two word processors, but, working with either of them for a while, you'll be reluctant to switch to the other. (You may think of this type of habit formation as a way of minimizing the transaction costs involved in switching.)

In short, there are many reasons to prefer something that we are used to, or already have, to something similar that is new. However, in the case of the coffee mug it is not clear that any of the explanations above is very compelling. There is relatively little uncertainty about the quality of the mug: mugs are mugs. The experiment does not allow us to switch among mugs, so that the second issue is not terribly relevant either. And finally, there isn't that much to get used to in using a mug to drink coffee. As a result, you may find that, while it is generally a good idea to stick to your choices to some extent, it isn't rational to demand for the mug much more than you are willing to pay in order to buy it.

It is important that we need not make a single decision in our life, whether we do or do not exhibit the endowment effect. It is quite possible that we will find the endowment effect rational for us in some cases but not in others. The following examples illustrate.

Mary is a 75-year-old woman who lives alone in a large house. When asked, why not sell it and move to an apartment that fits her needs better, she says, "Look, this is where I raised my children with my beloved husband. Every corner of the house is filled with memories. It is the story of my life." If you ask how much you need to pay Mary in order for her to sell the house, you'll find that the answer is much higher than the amount she would be willing to pay for another house of a similar size in a similar neighborhood.

Next consider Bob. Bob held a portfolio of real-estate stocks that went down considerably. Yet, Bob doesn't sell the stocks. When asked why, he says, "Well, this is a temporary blip. I believe they'll go up again." "Oh," you answer, "in this case why don't you buy more of these stocks?" "Are you nuts?" is Bob's reply, "buy *more* after I've lost so much on them?!"

I trust that you don't find Mary's behavior irrational. Her utility from owning the house cannot be summarized by the number of square feet she has at her disposal. Memories and emotions are part of the experience of "consuming" the house, and they exist only in this particular house. They cannot be traded or transferred. Therefore we should not be surprised that Mary evaluates her house, with her memories, rather differently from another house, even though the market finds them similar.

By contrast, Bob's behavior will probably be deemed less rational to most readers. In fact, this phenomenon has a name: the *disposition effect*.[9] People have been found to be reluctant to sell equities that went down in value. If Bob were to say, "You know, I've been an owner of stock XYZ for so long, it's like a friend to me," you'd consider him a bit sentimental for a rational investor. (Indeed, the disposition bias is not explained by an emotional relationship with the equity. Rather, it may have to do with the willingness to confront one's mistakes.)

Let us remind ourselves that what is rational for you always remains a matter of your judgment. While few people find framing effects rational, the endowment effect may well be rational, at least for some people in some circumstances. Many of the psychological biases we discuss here probably came into being because they make sense, and lead to good decisions, in some contexts. They are discussed here because in other contexts they may result in silly decisions. The name of the game is to ask ourselves in which situations a certain mode of behavior is rational for us, and in which situations it isn't. For each type of bias, each of us has to decide where to draw the rationality line, beyond which one decides to change one's behavior.

Sunk Costs

Problems 2.3 and 2.14 are similar: in both you have to decide whether to keep watching a disappointing movie or do something else. However, there is a slight difference between them. Problem 2.3 is:

> You go to a movie. It was supposed to be good, but it turns out to be boring. Would you leave in the middle and do something else instead?

Whereas Problem 2.14 reads:

> Your friend had a ticket to a movie. She couldn't make it, and gave you the ticket "instead of just throwing it away." The movie was supposed to be good, but it turns out to be boring. Would you leave in the middle and do something else instead?

While in Problem 2.3 it isn't specified how you got the ticket, the implicit assumption is that you bought it. Thus, the difference is that in Problem 2.3 you (presumably) paid for the ticket, and in

Problem 2.14 you didn't. Often, this difference results in different choices: people find it easier to walk out in the middle of a boring movie if they didn't pay for it than if they did.

Is this rational? Most economists would say that it isn't. The argument is obvious: once you're inside the movie theater, it doesn't make any difference whether you have or have not paid to get in. No one will give you your money back if you walk out. So, the reasoning goes, whatever the amount of money you invested to get the ticket, you should ignore it in your current decision. The amount of money you may have paid is a *sunk cost*, as it cannot be retrieved. And to many, rationality dictates that sunk costs be ignored.

If you accept this reasoning, you should ask yourself why many people sometimes find themselves behaving differently, that is, taking sunk costs into account. Are there any circumstances where it actually makes sense to do so? Or are there modes of behavior that are generally effective and useful, but that sometimes result in failing to ignore sunk costs?

You may be reminded of the status quo bias discussed above. If you had a plan to buy a ticket and to go to the movie, the status quo bias suggests that you should stay your course and stick to this plan rather than change it before it is completed. Some of the reasons that could justify the status quo bias might apply here as well. In particular, if you tend to follow your original plans, your decision making gains some stability. In our example, imagine that you sit there in the movie theater and contemplate your choice (the movie, as we agreed, is too boring anyway). So you say to yourself, "Well, I don't really like this movie. I should get out." But then another, more responsible voice inside your head replies, "OK, but then what? What will I do?" "Go see another movie" might be your bored-self reply. "Spend money on another ticket and go to see another movie? What is there to guarantee that I won't be disappointed again? Maybe this other movie, like this one, will look promising but will end up being boring too? I could go on switching like that from one theater to another all night long, spending tons of money and not enjoying anything. No, I'll be better off staying here. Maybe the movie will get more interesting…".

In other words, there is a danger that our evaluations of the options might change too much, and that switching to options that appear better may result in achieving nothing. Many of our decisions have to do with projects that take time; a movie is a relatively minor project, while education is a major one. What both have in common, however, is that a satisfactory outcome may require some effort over time, and we achieve very little from an unfinished project. Since we face the danger of too frequent switches, a bias for the completion of an already-started project may be beneficial in the long run.

There could be other explanations of the tendency to complete projects. One of them has to do with self-control. Let's go back to the dialog between you and yourself above, and assume that you say, petulantly, "But this movie is *boring!*" and your responsible self says, "Fine. So next time you should check what movie you're going to see *before* you buy the ticket. Now you stay here and this will teach you a lesson." In this case, the person is not a monolithic decision maker, but is better viewed as a collection of different players who have different goals. One of them is responsible for short-term fun, and another for long-term goals, such as being frugal. The discussion between them is reminiscent of the interaction between a child and a parent, where the latter is fully committed to the child's well-being, but believes this goal will be best served by forgoing some short-term temptations.

Yet another explanation would put the emphasis on the social aspect of one's decision. If you go to a movie and then leave in the middle, some people may suspect that you're impatient or unreliable in general. If you do it too often, and have such a reputation, people might hesitate to launch joint projects with you, thinking to themselves, "Sure, this person is all excited now, but what would happen if they changed their mind? Will I be left alone?" Along these lines, if you go to the movie with friends, you may have a good reason to take sunk costs into account: ignoring them might involve a slight embarrassment, an admission that you may regret your own choices, that you may drop unfinished projects, and so forth.

Observe that if the movie ticket was given to you by a friend who had no other use for it, all these justifications of staying in the movie theater are much weaker. Hence, these ways of thinking might explain why people sometimes behave differently in the two problems. But if you are on your own, with no one to impress, and you're quite sure that you'll be better off at home at this point, you may indeed be convinced that how much money you paid for the ticket is irrelevant: it is a sunk cost and should therefore have no impact on your current decision.

Decision Trees

If you wish to ignore sunk costs, how can you do that? One simple but useful technique is to model your decision problem as a decision tree. In such a tree you describe each decision by a node, where the tree branches out, leading to other nodes. If you have a multistage decision to make, you start with the first and then proceed to describe the other available decisions, *depending on the choices already made*. In Problem 2.3 the first choice is whether to buy a ticket to the movie, and then a subsequent choice, *in the case you did buy a ticket*, is whether to stay and watch the movie.

Some of the uncertainties we face are not up to us to decide about. They depend on random events or on other players. In our example, it is not known a priori whether the movie will be interesting or not. Such uncertainty can also be described by branching in the decision tree, only this time the branching node represents not your own decision, but someone else's. We often refer to "nature" as the player who makes these random choices. More generally, such nodes can be controlled either by other players, who are conscious decision makers like us, and who may be analyzing the same decision tree and thinking about our choices, or by nature. The crucial difference is that nature is not assumed to have well-defined goals, or a utility function; it chooses randomly, and we try to estimate the probabilities with which it may make any possible choice. When other players are involved, we will often know something about their goals and incentives, and will try to figure out what they might do, in any of their decision nodes, based on that knowledge. However, once we have figured out what these other players might do, or at least what are the probabilities that they would adopt each possible choice, we can think of these players and of nature as part of our environment. They control some decision nodes in our tree; their choices matter to us, but we can't dictate them.

A decision tree for Problem 2.3 might look as follows:

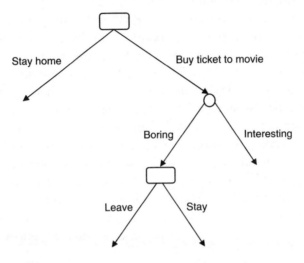

Decision tree 2.1.

The first node designates your original choice, whether to buy a ticket and go to the movie (right branch) or to stay home (left branch). Often such decision nodes are depicted as rectangles. If you make the latter choice, we are led to a subtree in which you stay home. We can further elaborate this subtree, describing various choices you have in it, such as to watch TV or read a book. At some point we will need to finish this description, and will write down the outcome of that path in the tree. Since in Problem 2.3 we already know that you bought a ticket, let's focus on the subtree on the right hand side. In it we get to a chance move, drawn here as a circle. It describes two eventualities that may unfold, as if these were two possible decisions, but this time they are nature's decisions, not yours. The decision is to make the movie boring or interesting. Observe that you need not think of this as an actual decision made by any superpower. Moreover, whether the movie would be boring or interesting was probably determined long ago. However, as far as you are concerned, this is an uncertainty that has not been resolved until you actually buy the ticket and go to see the movie. Hence we can draw the two possible resolutions of this uncertainty as two branches coming out of the circle as if nature were making this decision right there and then.

If nature decides to make the movie interesting, and we're led down the rightmost path, you obtain the outcome of watching an interesting movie. If, however, nature decides to make the movie boring, as we know it did in Problem 2.3, we're going down the path that leads left from the circle (nature's node). And then we are finally faced with the decision problem in 2.3: having bought a ticket, and having found that the movie is boring, now you have to choose between leaving and staying. To keep the diagram simple, I have omitted the outcomes that should appear in each leaf of the tree.

Let us now consider Problem 2.14. Decision tree 2.2 shows how that problem might look. The only difference between decision trees 2.2 and 2.1 is that the former involves no payment for the ticket, whereas the latter does. This difference should be reflected in the

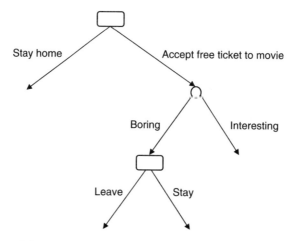

Decision tree 2.2.

outcomes at the leaves of both trees: having paid for the ticket, you will have less money than if you had got it for free. Therefore, if we compare the subtrees that describe the Leave/Stay decisions in the two decision trees, they are not quite the same: they do describe the same choices, and the outcomes are the same, but in one subtree all outcomes have the same amount of money deducted from them. However, the choice between Leave and Stay should probably not be affected by this difference, as none of the money you paid in Problem 2.3 will be reimbursed to you. Hence, many people feel that the choice in the two problems should be identical. And if you use a decision tree to make your choices, you are more likely to focus on the relevant subtree and ignore sunk costs.[10]

If the subtrees in the two decision trees were completely identical (also in terms of the exact outcome at each leaf), the claim that the same decision should be made in both problems would have been even more compelling. In this case it follows, from a principle that is sometimes called *consequentialism*, that your decision in a subtree should only depend on that subtree. If I accept this principle, then, having arrived at a certain decision node, I can forget about all the other parts of the tree, including the path that led me to where I am, and all the other branches that could have materialized but didn't. Rather, my current choice should depend only on the options available to me now and the future choices and outcomes they might lead to.

If you decide to use decision trees, and you commit to consequentialism, you will be less prone to sunk-cost effects, as well as to other phenomena that people sometimes feel uncomfortable about. For example, no one likes to experience regret. Yet, people often feel that they should focus on the future options available to them, rather than think about what they could have done but didn't. In particular, many people find it irrational to give up on material payoff only in order to avoid the experience of regret. Decision trees, coupled with consequentialism, can help you avoid these modes of behavior: whatever choices you could have made belong to other subtrees, different than the one you're facing. Hence the payoffs you could have received there are immaterial, and should not affect your current choice.

People often find it rational to ignore counterfactuals, namely, eventualities that would have unfolded were reality different than it is, and consequentialism helps you do that. But consequentialism also means that you ignore the path that led you to the subtree you are facing. That is, not only counterfactual, hypothetical worlds are ignored, but also actual history, to the extent that it does not affect future outcomes. Isn't this a bit extreme? Does it mean, for example, that you should be ungrateful to your old teachers or your parents, if they do not affect outcomes in the remaining subtree?

Well, this would be your conclusion if by "outcome" you think only about monetary payoff, and your past benefactors no longer have any effects on these payoffs. But this is a rather restrictive way of looking at decision problems. The outcome of a tree also specifies other things that matter to you, such as the well-being of your loved ones, and your own emotional reactions. Hence, consequentialism need not make you a heartless bastard – it all depends on what is incorporated in the outcomes.

Wait a minute, you may say: if you start getting all kinds of emotional phenomena into the outcomes, what would prevent me from putting regret in as well? And then consequentialism will not rule out regret, or sunk-cost effects, and, in fact, it's not clear it will rule out anything! This is a very valid point. However, if you use a decision tree it will be clear to you to what extent past and counterfactual choices affect your behavior. If they do, you will find yourself either violating consequentialism, or writing down outcomes that explicitly take these considerations into account. And this will help you make decisions in a way that is rational for you.

Representativeness Heuristic

Problems 2.4 and 2.15 are identical. You were asked to rank the following statements about Linda:

a. Linda is a teacher in an elementary school.
b. Linda works in a bookstore and takes yoga classes.
c. Linda is active in a feminist movement.
d. Linda is a psychiatric social worker.
e. Linda is a member of the League of Women Voters.

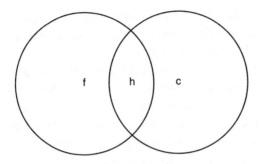

Figure 2.1 Venn diagram showing (h) as the intersection of (f) and (c).

f. Linda is a bank teller.
g. Linda is an insurance salesperson.
h. Linda is a bank teller who is active in a feminist movement.

The point is to see if you ranked (f) as less likely than (h). Typically, I get 40–50% of the class exhibiting this ranking. However, upon careful inspection, everyone agrees that it doesn't make sense to rank (f) as less likely than (h), because (h) is fully contained in (f). That is, there is no way in which (h) will occur without (f) occurring as well. In fact, (h) is the intersection[11] of (f) and (c) (Figure 2.1). So what's going on in this example? Why do many people rank (h) as more likely than (f) even though, after a moment's reflection, they agree that this ranking does not make sense?

The answers here vary. First, many people argue that when they read (f) they didn't understand it to mean "Linda is a bank teller, who may or may not be active in a feminist movement," but "Linda is a bank teller who is *not* active in a feminist movement." That is, they argue that they understood (f) in the context of (h), and this context, "not active in a feminist movement," was implicitly understood, though not stated.

While this is quite possible, there is no reason to understand (f) in this sense, especially as it is stated before (h). But this is not so important. The point of this example, as well as other examples you may consider irrational, is not to make you feel stupid. The point is to highlight certain biases that most of us are prone to, in the hope that, with awareness and some analysis, you will exhibit only those biases you feel comfortable with.

So let's move on to the second explanation. This explanation is due to Kahneman and Tversky, who developed this and similar examples and used them in experiments.[12] They referred to these examples as the *conjunction fallacy*, because in them the conjunction of two events is ranked as more plausible than one of the events. Kahneman and Tversky offered the following explanation of the conjunction fallacy.

In everyday as well as professional life we are bombarded with judgment and evaluation questions. Alas, often there isn't sufficient information on which to base a carefully reasoned answer to the question at hand. In the case above, we are asked to rank eight statements. This can be viewed as replying to 28 questions about the relative likelihood of pairs of statements. Only two pairs ((c) and (h), and (f) and (h)) can be ranked based on logic and probability alone. Assuming you don't have access to the relevant statistical data, 26 out of the 28 pairs are left unranked if you restrict yourself to carefully argued answers. In other words, relying on logic and probability often leaves us with no answer.

What do we do? According to Kahneman and Tversky, the human mind has developed "heuristics." These are methods of generating answers that are not guaranteed to provide a correct answer, but that do result in plausible answers most of the time. For instance, in the problem above, Kahneman and Tversky argued that people use "representativeness heuristic," which suggests that we ask ourselves what is representative, or typical, of Linda. Given Linda's description, being a bank teller seems at odds with her image. Hence (f) is deemed unlikely. By contrast, being a bank teller who is active in a feminist movement is "more like Linda." It is easier for us to imagine how this fits Linda: for instance, she had to take a job as a bank teller to make a living, but in her spare time she continued to support the causes she felt passionately about.

Importantly, representativeness heuristic makes sense most of the time. If I were to ask you whether Linda were more likely to be active in a feminist movement or a pro-life (anti-abortion) movement, you would probably vote for the feminist movement, and this would probably be supported by statistical data (if we could get them). That is, representativeness heuristic, like other heuristics we will consider later on, is not stupid. To the contrary: it is a useful and reasonable way of providing answers to difficult problems. But sometimes it may lead us astray, as this example illustrates. According to this view, it's a good idea to be aware of our biases and of the heuristics our minds use, and it's also a good idea to ask why they are, on the whole, useful. At the same time, we would like to know when these reasoning techniques, which are generally successful, might lead to wrong answers.

There are other stories that can be told about the particular example of Linda. For instance, one might argue that the very task that we are asked to perform in this problem is not very natural: very seldom do we find ourselves ranking statements according to their relative likelihood. By contrast, a task that we perform on a daily basis is judging whether our interlocutor is honest. When we have to deal with this doubt, an abundance of details that do not contradict each other makes the speaker more likely to be truth telling. This is basically what happens when a witness is cross-examined in court: the witness is asked about various details. The more they talk and the more statements they utter, the lower is the probability that all these statements are true (by the same logic that says that (h) cannot be more likely than (f)). But if the witness survives a long cross-examination with no apparent contradictions, we tend to believe that they are telling the truth. The reason is that we judge the probability not of the statements themselves, but of the event that the witness is not lying. And longer statements that are consistent arouse more faith than shorter ones.

By a similar logic, assume that, a few years after you last saw Linda, I tell you that I have just met her. You ask me what she's up to these days, and I provide one of the answers (a)–(h). Even if you have no doubt that I'm telling the truth, you are still aware of the fact that there's more than one Linda in this world, and there's some doubt in your mind whether the Linda I met is indeed the same Linda you once knew. In this set-up, you won't be trying to assess the probability that the statement I make is true of Linda, given that this is the same Linda; rather, you'll be asking yourself what is the probability that this is the same Linda, given what the statement says. And then, with a sufficient number of details that are typical of Linda, you may be convinced that this is the same Linda even if you never expected her to be a bank teller. According to this story, when people are asked to rank the eight statements, the answers they provide are not sheer like-lihood judgments of the statements presented, because they are colored by the answers to other questions such as "Is this person tell-ing me the truth?" or "Are we talking about the same Linda?"

Be that as it may, the conjunction fallacy is an impressive phenom-enon, which makes an important point: it is useful to use representa-tiveness heuristic, but it can sometimes lead to wrong judgments and therefore also to wrong decisions, where, as always, "wrong" is subjectively understood. Linda's example is another one that will not survive a formal model: if we use the machinery of probability theory to represent our beliefs, we will find it impossible to assign a lower probability to an event (f) than to a subevent thereof (h).

Linda the bank teller has become a very famous example. Some studies which tried to replicate the findings of Kahneman and Tversky didn't obtain as strong an effect as the original study. Indeed, it has been argued that Kahneman and Tversky's examples were carefully chosen, and that some of the effects they found were more dramatic in laboratory experiments than they would be in real life.[13]

The debate regarding the scope and implications of the findings of Kahneman and Tversky and their followers is still active, and will probably remain so for years to come. As mentioned in the introduc-tion, the conclusions the psychologists, economists, and decision theorists reach on these issues are important for our descriptive use of the theory: we might want to know which model best describes the behavior of decision makers around us. However, this debate is less relevant for normative applications. For these we would like to see in which ways we can improve our own decision making. Hence I try to provide convincing examples (typically, the original examples used by Kahneman and Tversky and their colleagues and followers), asking whether you can find yourself making a certain decision. The next question is whether you like making decisions this way. If the answer to both questions is negative, we are dealing with a mode of behavior that you find silly, but that, luckily, is not a mode you may find yourself adopting. If the answer to both questions is positive, then you might not be rational by the standards of some economists, but you are happy with your own decisions. If, however, the answer to the first question is positive and to the second question negative, we're dealing with a case in which you may improve your decision making in your own eyes. Understanding such examples is the main goal of this book.

Availability Heuristic

Problems 2.5 and 2.16 are quite similar. They read:

> In four pages of a novel (about 2,000 words) in English, do you expect to find more than 10 words that have the form
> [Problem 2.5:] _ _ _ _ _ _ n _ (seven-letter words that have the letter n in the sixth position)?
> [Problem 2.16:] _ _ _ _ *ing* (seven-letter words that end with *ing*)?

The typical finding is that the second formulation results in higher estimates than the first. This doesn't seem very logical, because the first problem describes a larger set of words than the second: every seven-letter word that ends with "ing" is a seven-letter word that has "n" in the penultimate position.

Why do people give higher estimates for the "ing" ending as compared with all the endings "ana," "anb," "anc"... combined? The reason seems obvious: when asked a question such as this, we probe our minds, and try to think of examples of the type discussed. Clearly, if I had a list with all the seven-letter words I know in English and I tried to assess the frequency of appearance of each one of them, and then sum up these frequencies, I would never come up with a higher estimate for "ing" than for "_n_". Similarly, if I had a computer doing these statistics for me, again, the estimate for the "_n_" ending would have to be at least as large as the estimate for the "ing" ending. But I do not have a computer to calculate this for me, nor is it very practical for me to try to think of all the seven-letter words I know. So I do the best I can. I try to imagine words of the type involved. And then it may be a little difficult to think of words that end with "_n_", but it is much easier to think of words that end with "ing". When I ask you to think of the latter, I restrict the set of words you're allowed to use as examples. But I also give you a hint as to how to generate such words.

Kahneman and Tversky referred to this phenomenon as *availability heuristic*.[14] Basically, it can be thought of as a heuristic to solve likelihood estimation problems. In the absence of a carefully maintained and easily accessible database, we sample our own memory for examples – and certain examples that are more easily available to us will have a higher weight in the resulting estimate. It is as if we were taking a biased sample: in trying to recall cases, or to imagine scenarios, those that are more conspicuous, or more available, will have a higher probability of being sampled, and the resulting sample may not be representative of the target population.

Problems 2.6 and 2.17 make a similar point.[15] The first reads:

What is the probability that, in the next two years, there will be a cure for AIDS?

Whereas the second:

What is the probability that, in the next two years, there will be a new genetic discovery in the study of apes, and a cure for AIDS?

The second problem thus deals with a more specific event. If you are considering both events simultaneously, you should not assign a higher probability to the second event than to the first: any scenario that satisfies the condition "there will be a new genetic discovery in the study of apes, and a cure for AIDS" also satisfies the condition "in the next two years, there will be a cure for AIDS," just as any word that ends with "ing" also ends with "_n_". But the discovery in the study of apes suggests a way in which the event can occur, and thereby makes it more available to your mind, just as the "hint" of "ing" suggests a way in which a word might end with "_n_". Thus, if you ponder Problem 2.6, you may be thinking, "Oh, this is a long shot. They've been looking for a cure for such a long time, why would they find one now?" But when you read Problem 2.17, you might say to yourself, "I do remember some story about AIDS starting with a blood transfusion from apes. It makes sense that the cure would come from there!"

Next consider Problems 2.7 and 2.18. In the former you are asked:

What is the probability that, during the next year, your car could be a "total loss" due to an accident?

Whereas in the latter:

What is the probability that, during the next year, your car could be a "total loss" due to:

a. An accident in which the other driver is drunk?
b. An accident for which you are responsible?
c. An accident occurring while your car is parked on the street?
d. An accident occurring while your car is parked in a garage?
e. One of the above?

We would like to compare the answer to (e) in Problem 2.18 with the answer to Problem 2.7. Typically, the former exceeds the latter, often by much. The reason is probably related to availability heuristic again: while Problem 2.7 only asks for the probability of an event, Problem 2.18 offers many ways in which the accident could happen. If we were restricting attention to one item out of (a)–(d) in Problem 2.18, the formal structure would have been the same as in the previous example (comparing Problems 2.6 and 2.17). In this case the effect is used to "magnify" an evaluated probability. Since availability heuristics makes each of the scenarios (a)–(d) in Problem 2.18 more conspicuous than it was in Problem 2.7, the addition over all of them results in a larger estimate.

In various studies of this nature, it was found that *unpacking* an event, or breaking it into several subevents, could result in magnifying its assessed probability by a factor of 1.5 or more.[16] You might have had the experience of buying an insurance policy, with an agent who tries to sell an insurance against various types of risk. After you've insured yourself against some risks, the agent might go on and describe in very vivid colors the next type of calamity, against which you haven't yet bought insurance. It is as if the insurance agent makes you think about Problem 2.18 rather than Problem 2.7. As is generally the case, a psychological bias that can be used to make money has already been discovered by practitioners.

This example is interesting for another reason as well. Consider the two problems again, and ask yourself: where do you believe you would give a better assessment of the true probability of your car being a total loss – in the itemized version (Problem 2.18) or the bottom-line-only version (Problem 2.7)? It is quite possible that you were more accurate in the bottom-line-only version, because the itemized version made you overestimate the probability of the event. If this is the case, this is an example where thinking more might result in less-good answers. The reason is that in the itemized version we are led to think a lot about the way the event (total loss) could happen, but we don't devote similar attention to the complementary event, that is, that the car is not lost. It is not obvious how one can split one's time, thinking about various scenarios, in an "even-handed way," devoting the same amount of time to events that are equally likely. Indeed, this is precisely the problem of assigning probabilities to these scenarios. But it is obvious that itemizing only one event introduces a bias. Importantly, we find that sometimes "thinking more" isn't "thinking better," and consequently sometimes the intuitive, gut feeling answer will be better than the reasoned one.

Our final example of availability heuristic is Problem 2.8 (identical to Problem 2.19):

Which of the following causes more deaths?

a. Digestive diseases.
b. Motor vehicle accidents.

Most people tend to choose (b). The data that I have available (no pun intended) is for 2002.[17] In this year, the answer was (a), with digestive diseases causing more than 50% more deaths than motor vehicle accidents. To be precise, for each death by motor vehicle accident, there were 1.66 deaths by digestive diseases. However, we suspect that the numbers of media reports about deaths of each type would give us a very different ratio.

This example highlights the nature of availability heuristic as a biased sample: you are asked to compare the probability of the two types of death, but you probably don't have the data needed for such a comparison. You still have to make a judgment. So you try to think, and probe for examples from memory. Most of the deaths you know about come from the media. And if the media is biased in its reports, there is no wonder that the "sample" you carry around with you in your memory is biased as well.

Observe that we're not in the business of media-bashing here. The point is not that journalists only seek sensational headlines. In fact, it makes a lot of sense to report on traffic accidents: they are avoidable. If we hear about them in the media, maybe we'll drive more carefully and lives will be saved. By contrast, public awareness does not suffice to avoid deaths caused by digestive diseases. Awareness always helps, but it is surely easier to save lives in the case of traffic accidents. As a result, the media is serving an important social goal by reporting (easily avoidable) traffic accident deaths more often than (less avoidable) disease victims. Yet, it is useful to recall that this social goal introduces a bias into the sample generated by media reports.

Anchoring

Problems 2.9 and 2.20 were quite similar:

> A newly hired engineer for a computer firm in Melbourne, Australia, has four years of experience and good all-round quali fications.
> Do you think that her annual salary is above or below [Problem 2.9: $65,000; Problem 2.20: $135,000]?
> What is your estimate of her salary?

Typically, there is a statistically significant difference between the answers given in the two conditions. And, as you can guess, people give higher estimates if they are first asked about the higher value.

This is an example of the *anchoring effect*.[18] It is the effect that irrelevant, or nearly irrelevant, information might have, above and beyond what can be reasonably justified. In Kahneman and Tversky's original examples the information was the assessment provided by someone else, who was declared to know very little about the problem at hand. The point is that, in the absence of sound data, your assessment may be affected by almost arbitrary pieces of information even if their relevance is rather limited.

The anchoring effect derives from an anchoring heuristic, postulated to be employed in the assessment of unknown quantities with very little information: you begin with some estimate, which serves as an "anchor," and you correct it. Thus, if you're told that someone estimated the salary at $65,000, this is the anchor. Then you think some more and may conclude that this is actually too low, so you correct upwards. But even after the correction the estimate is likely to be lower than it would have been had you started with $135,000 as your anchor.

In the examples used here, I changed the anchor: rather than it being an explicit estimate given by someone else, it is only a question. This is designed to minimize the actual information that is being given by the anchor: here information is not explicitly given, as the anchors ($65,000 and $135,000) are only mentioned as part of a question. This does not mean that they convey no information. The very fact that these values were chosen to be asked about may tell you something. But it is arguably less relevant than a number which is given explicitly as someone else's assessment.

Is anchoring rational? Do you like the fact that your answers might vary with the anchors provided? The answer is not obvious. As we have just said, anchoring cannot be dismissed simply as a mistake. An assessment provided by someone, however poorly informed, is still an assessment. And if you have a theory about the people who pose questions and why they should pose certain questions rather than others, then their choice of questions is also informative. Yet, you may not feel comfortable with the fact that your assessment varies with information that may be arbitrary. Moreover, you may worry about the fact that this information can be used strategically.

Consider the following example. An employee is being reviewed by a committee, which can decide to discontinue employment, continue under current terms, or promote the employee. You walk into the meeting and say "I really feel that this person should be promoted." Later on, when you're asked to support your opinion, it may turn out that you don't have very convincing arguments, and your colleagues don't vote for promotion. But the very fact that promotion was mentioned and discussed is a sort of anchor, and it may make the continuation of employment a non-issue. By contrast, if you start off by suggesting that employment be discontinued, even if you have no arguments to support that view, you may find that promotion is barely discussed.

In real life it may be hard to identify cases of pure anchoring effects. In the promotion example above, your colleagues might start from your position out of courtesy. People may have an incentive to avoid conflict, and therefore refrain from promoting a view that's very different from the one already stated. Conversely, they may also be antagonistic and seek an opposing view intentionally. Anchoring effects often interact with strategic considerations of these types.

Mental Accounting

Problem 2.10 read:

> You have bought a ticket to a concert, which cost you $50. When you arrive at the concert hall, you find you have lost the ticket. Would you buy another one (assuming you have enough money in your wallet)?

And Problem 2.21:

> You are going to a concert. Tickets cost $50. When you arrive at the concert hall, you find you have lost a $50 bill. Would you still buy the ticket (assuming you have enough money in your wallet)?

Typically, people tend to respond in the affirmative (for buying a ticket) more in the second case than in the first. The reasoning is, roughly, that in the second case the $50 bill has nothing to do with the concert. By contrast, in the first case you'd already spent $50 on the concert, and lost the ticket, and now you're about to spend even more. Some people say, "$100 on this concert is really too much to spend."

However, standard economic reasoning would suggest that the decision in the two cases should be the same. Suppose that you start with $m + 50$ dollars. In Problem 2.10 you bought a ticket, and were left with m dollars. We can think of the purchase as exchanging the bundle $(m + 50, 0)$ for $(m, 1)$, where the first coordinate is the amount of money you have, and the second coordinate the number of tickets. Alas, having lost the ticket you find that rather than $(m, 1)$ you have $(m, 0)$. Now the question is whether you prefer this bundle to buying a ticket, that is, which is preferred:

$$(m, 0) \text{ or } (m - 50, 1)$$

In the second case, you started with the bundle $(m + 50, 0)$ and, before having bought the ticket, managed to lose $50. So now you have only (*m*, 0). Again, the question is whether you'd stick to this bundle (giving up on the concert), or buy the ticket and have (*m* − 50, 1). That is, it is precisely the same question.

Standard economic modeling does not allow us to treat the two cases differently. We can imagine a situation in which a person won't buy the second ticket, because they won't be left with enough money to buy food. But then they won't buy the ticket in both cases, whether what they have lost was a ticket or a $50 bill. Similarly, they may shrug their shoulders and buy the ticket, because they can afford to. But then this should be their decision in both cases. A decision tree might help them see that the ticket and the $50 bill are sunk costs, leaving them with precisely the same material payoff in the subtree you're facing.

The standard economic assumption is that money is fungible: a dollar is a dollar is a dollar. Dollars don't come with name tags on them; they can be transferred from one expense to another. However, Richard Thaler argued, using examples as above, that people have *mental accounts*:[19] even though money is indeed fungible, people often behave as if a certain sum "belongs" to a certain class of expenditures.

Another example suggested by Thaler is the following.[20] Mr Smith goes by a store and sees a sweater. He likes it, but decides that it's too expensive to buy. When he comes home, he finds that his wife bought him precisely the same sweater for his birthday, and he's happy. If the couple has only joint bank accounts, how can the man be pleased to see that his wife made precisely the decision he decided not to make?

A birthday present from one's spouse differs from one's own spontaneous decision in two ways. One is agency, namely, who makes the decision (and bears the responsibility for it). When the wife buys the sweater, she relieves her husband from the responsibility for the decision. If he were to buy it himself, he would need to justify the purchase to himself, and perhaps to cope with the blow to his self-image as a frugal person.

The second difference is the occasion of the birthday. If the sweater comes out of the "birthday account," it is a legitimate expense. This account has a certain budget, and as long as all birthday presents do not exceed it, everything's fine. Observe that this could work even if we ignored the agency issues: the man can decide to buy a present to himself, and feel that it is fine to do so on his birthday, but not on any other day.

Why do we observe mental accounting? When can it be useful? There are at least three distinct explanations of this phenomenon:

a. *Complexity:* Consider the government budget. Taking a rather idealized view of a complex organization, let us think of the government as a single decision maker who has a well-defined utility function. It considers all possible expenses, on schools and roads, hospitals and police, and strikes a trade-off that does the most good to the citizens (or so one should hope). Assume now that a certain bridge suddenly collapses. There is an unpredictable new expense. Since the overall budget has decreased, the optimization problem should be re-solved. In particular, the extra expense of fixing the bridge might have to be shared by all departments. Maybe the hospitals should buy less medication, or the schools should give up some computers. In principle, the government should get together again and determine what the new budget should be. But it is not very practical to re-allocate the budget every time a bridge collapses. The complexity of the government's budget problem precludes a perfect re-optimization, and calls for a simplifying approach: divide the budget among major categories, divide each category into subcategories, allocate the budget to these, and so on. In each subcategory one needs to consider only transfers between items in this subcategory. This means that there are relatively few comparisons to be made, and they tend to be between subcategories that are similar in nature. Hence, the problem becomes much easier.

   Considering an individual consumer again, we observe that for most people the budget allocation problem is also quite complex. This may not be true if you have to survive on $10 a day, and your basic needs already exhaust your budget without leaving you too many choices. But if you're fortunate enough to have a much higher income, there is a multitude of ways in which you could spend your budget. How would you decide? How could you even conceive of all the consumption bundles that are available to you? This problem is akin to the government's budget problem, and you may adopt a similar approach: start by allocating your income among major categories, such as food, housing, entertainment, and so forth. Within each category, you can go on to divide the budget into subcategories, and so on. As a result, you have money that you have decided is allocated to certain types of expenses, that is, a mental accounting system.

b. *Self-control:* Consider Mr Smith who sees the sweater that he would like to have. The sweater is not cheap, but he can afford to buy it. However, Mr Smith says to himself, "What would happen if I were to buy such luxury items whenever I feel like it? Today it will be a sweater, tomorrow a leather bag, and at the end of the month I'll discover a huge bill on my credit card." "No," he responds to himself, "it's only this once. I'll buy the sweater and as of tomorrow I'll be as frugal as a monk." "Com'n," he continues his internal debate, still by the store's window, "it's easy to say 'just this once' – I can say the same thing tomorrow and then the day after tomorrow. It's going to be like the story with this diet that I always begin the following Monday…".

Thus, Mr Smith is coping with a problem of self-control. He's sophisticated enough to realize that he's prone to break his own promises to himself. One way to help himself resist the temptation is to decide, at the beginning of the month, how much he's going to spend on each category of products, and do his best not to exceed that. Of course, in the absence of a commitment device he may also fail to respect this promise. But keeping track of the expenses in each category may alleviate the self-control problem: at least there will be a red light blinking when he spends too much.

c. *Memory:* A related problem one may have is of recording small purchases. Assume that Jane made a decision to consume wine every day, but to limit herself, most of the time, to $10 bottles.

She figured out that she can have a $30 bottle about 15% of the times, but no more than that. So she says to herself, "Great, I'll buy wine, at $10 or $30 a bottle, and I just have to make sure that the number of times I buy the more expensive bottles doesn't exceed 54 per year."

Obviously, this is going to be difficult to implement, even if Jane has no self-control problems. The implementation of her consumption strategy requires not only iron will, but also perfect memory. If she can't quite remember how many times she bought the more expensive bottle this year, she might buy it too often, or she might be unduly cautious and drink cheap wine more often than she could have afforded to. One possible solution is to use the calendar as a memory aid: Jane can decide to have a more expensive bottle on Saturday nights, and a less expensive one the rest of the week. Thus, she need not keep track of her past consumption – she only needs to obey the calendar. This is similar to Mr Smith's birthday gift: allowing oneself to spend more money on one's birthday is a way to enjoy some luxury from time to time, without fearing that one would end up spending too much (or too little) due to forgetfulness.

Similar phenomena occur when people consider large, non-repetitive expenses. People who are frugal on a daily basis may find themselves spending money much more easily when they are on a vacation, or when they move to a new house, and so on. In the case of the vacation, this may be due to the desire to make it a perfect experience. But this explanation doesn't seem compelling in the moving example. It is possible, however, that on a rather unique occasion such as moving, one doesn't have to worry about the higher expenses becoming a habit.

With all these explanations, it might seem that there is hardly anything more rational than mental accounting. But this is not what I am trying to say. As is the case with most psychological biases discussed here, there are many situations in which they lead to better decisions, and then there are others when they do not. Mental accounting is no exception: there are situations, as in the case of the lost ticket we started out with, where you may find that it is irrational to treat money as if it had a pre-destined use. Where to draw the line between useful and silly mental accounting remains, as always, your subjective choice.

Dynamic Inconsistency

Problem 2.11 asks you to compare

    a. Receiving $10 today.
    b. Receiving $12 a week from today.

Whereas Problem 2.22 asks you to compare

    a. Receiving $10 fifty weeks from today.
    b. Receiving $12 fifty-one weeks from today.

Often, more people choose option (a) in the first problem than in the second.[21] Moreover, there are many people who simultaneously choose (a) in Problem 2.11 and (b) in Problem 2.22. Is there any difficulty with such a pattern of choices? Well, maybe. Assume that you look at Problem 2.22 and decide to go for (b). Indeed, you say to yourself, it's anyway very far in the future. Whether I have to wait 50 weeks or 51 weeks, I have to be patient. But then why not get a 20% higher sum? However, assume that someone asks you, after 50 weeks have gone by, whether you'd like to change your choice. Now, "50 weeks" means "immediately," and "51 weeks" means "a week from now." That is, if you get the chance to change your choice, you are now facing the same choices as in Problem 2.11, and (assuming consequentialism) switch to (a).

If these are indeed the choices you make, you will be *dynamically inconsistent*: you will be making some choices about your future behavior, but, when the time comes to implement them, you will not want to. There are many problems of this nature. You may have to study for an exam, and you prefer to first go out with friends and study tomorrow. When tomorrow becomes today, you may again wish to postpone studying. In the end you may find yourself unprepared for the exam, which is not the choice you would have liked to make at the outset. Similarly, you may find yourself postponing the beginning of your savings, or your diet, or any other unpleasant choice that you are tempted to put off until a later date.

Dynamically inconsistent decision makers may be aware of their inconsistency, and take it into account. In particular, they may seek commitment devices that will limit their future choices and not allow them to deviate from their chosen course of action. For example, in the United States people used to join "Christmas Clubs" which were savings plans, yielding low or negative interest, and providing the benefit of one not being able to withdraw one's own money. The idea was that by putting your money in such a plan you can guarantee yourself that, no matter what happens during the year, and no matter how tempted you might be to do other things with your money, you will not be able to use it until Christmas, when you presumably need it to buy Christmas gifts.

The idea that, in the face of self-control problems, one might be better off with less choice dates back to Homer's *Odyssey*: Odysseus wants to enjoy the singing of the sirens, but not to be tempted by them. Knowing that he will not be able to resist the temptation, he orders his men to tie him to the boat's mast. This way he ends up enjoying the sirens' singing but also getting safely away from their island.

Self-control problems abound. They appear in the context of the consumption of addictive substances (including alcohol and tobacco), of the choice of diet and exercise, as well as of consumption habits and the accumulation of debt. When consumers are prone to self-control problems and may therefore be dynamically inconsistent, we cannot model them as coherent utility-maximizing agents. And this casts doubt on the validity of the arguments supporting free markets. In particular, these problems may justify regulations that limit people's choices, as in the cases of accumulating credit card debt, withdrawing from (or borrowing against) one's retirement funds, and so forth.[22]

Exercises

1. Some people are afraid of flying. They are often surprised to learn that many more people lose their lives in motor vehicle accidents (on the ground) than in airplanes. Why are their evaluations of these numbers inaccurate? And does it follow that flying is less dangerous than driving?

    _____

    _____

    _____

2. Jim and Joe are students who live on small scholarships. They go to an all-you-can-eat restaurant and pay $8.95 for the meal. Joe is unexpectedly told that, being the 100th customer of the day, he gets his money back (and gets to eat at no charge). Other things being equal, do you think that Joe will consume the same amount of food as Jim?

    _____

    _____

    _____

3. Magazines often offer their new customers a subscription over an initial period at a very low cost. Provide at least two reasons why this may be a smart way to attract customers.

    _____

    _____

    _____

4. Credit card companies used to offer students loans at enticing rates. Presumably, this was an example of voluntary trade

among adults, which should be allowed in a free market. Provide a reason why such offers may be restricted by law.

_____

_____

_____

5. In most countries, a driver who wishes to join an organ donation program has to make an explicit choice to do so. There is a proposal to make every driver an organ donor unless they opt out.[23] Do you think this proposal might have an effect on the number of organ donors? If so, which psychological effect might be responsible for this?

_____

_____

_____

6. Mary noticed that, when she gets an unexpected bonus from her employer, she allows herself to buy goods she didn't plan to buy, and often ends up spending an amount of money larger than her bonus. What psychological effect is related to this phenomenon, and what goes wrong in her decision making?

_____

_____

_____

Notes

1   See, for instance, Gigerenzer, G. and Hoffrage, U. (1995) How to improve Bayesian reasoning without instructions: frequency formats. *Psychological Review*, 102, 684–704.

2   Gigerenzer has been arguing that simple heuristics and intuition lead to rather good decisions in naturally occurring situations. See Gigerenzer, G. and Todd, P. M. (1999) *Simple Heuristics that Makes Us Smart*. Oxford University Press.

3   Tversky, A. and Kahneman, D. (1981) The framing of decisions and the psychology of choice. *Science*, 211, 453–458.

4   Lorge, I. and Solomon, H. (1955) Two models of group behavior in the solution of Eureka-type problems. *Psychometrika*, 20, 139–148; Davis, J. H. (1992) Some compelling intuitions about group consensus decisions, theoretical and empirical research, and interpersonal aggregation phenomena: selected examples, 1950–1990. *Organizational Behavior and Human Decision Processes*, 52, 3–38; Cooper, D. J. and Kagel, J. (2005) Are two heads better than one? Team versus individual play in signaling games. *American Economic Review*, 95, 477–509.

5   I'm blithely ignoring here the question of what a formal model is. In fact, what is formal enough for one may not be formal to another. More importantly, formal models may capture representations as well. But such models still force us to explicitly state all considerations that we allow to have an effect over our decisions.

6   Thaler, R. (1980) Toward a positive theory of consumer choice. *Journal of Economic Behavior and Organization*, 1, 39–60.

7   Samuelson, W. and Zeckhauser, R. J. (1988) Status quo bias in decision making. *Journal of Risk and Uncertainty*, 1, 7–59; Kahneman, D., Knetsch, J. L. & Thaler, R. H. (1991) Anomalies: the endowment effect, loss aversion, and status quo bias. *Journal of Economic Perspectives*, 5, 193–206.

8   Kahneman, D., Knetsch, J. L. & Thaler, R. H. (1990) Experimental test of the endowment effect and the Coase theorem. *Journal of Political Economy*, 98, 1325–1328.

9   Shefrin, H. and Statman, M. (1985) The disposition to sell winners too early and ride losers too long: theory and evidence. *Journal of Finance*, 3, 777–790.

10 If the amount of money lost is significant, so that it changes the available choices in the future, you are surely not expected to ignore it. But in this case we will not refer to it as sunk cost.

11 See Appendix B for basic definitions of operations on events.

12 Kahneman, D. and Tversky, A. (1972) Subjective probability: a judgment of representativeness. *Cognitive Psychology*, 3, 430–454; Tversky, A. and Kahneman, D. (1983) Extensional versus intuitive reasoning: the conjunction fallacy in probability judgments. *Psychological Review*, 90, 293–315.

13 Gigerenzer and Hoffrage (1995), see note 1.
14 Tversky, A. and Kahneman, D. (1973) Availability: a heuristic for judging frequency and probability. *Cognitive Psychology*, 5, 207–232; Tversky and Kahneman (1983), see note 12.
15 Tversky and Kahneman (1973), see note 14.
16 In some studies the factor exceeded 4. See Tversky, A. and Kohler, D. J. (1994) Support theory: a nonextensional representation of subjective probability. *Psychological Review*, 101, 547–567; Rottenstreich, Y. and Tversky, A. (1997) Unpacking, repacking, and anchoring: advances in support theory. *Psychological Review*, 104, 406–415. However, see also Sloman, S., Rottenstreich, Y., Wisniewski, E., Hadjichristidis, C. and Fox, C. (2004) Typical versus atypical unpacking and superadditive probability judgment. *Journal of Experimental Psychology: Learning, Memory, and Cognition*, 30, 573–582.
17 World Health Organization as quoted in Wikipedia, http://en.wikipedia.org/wiki/List_of_causes_of_death_by_rate.
18 Tversky, A. and Kahneman, D. (1974) Judgment under uncertainty: heuristics and biases. *Science*, 185, 1124–1131.
19 Thaler (1980), see note 6; Thaler, R. (1985) Mental accounting and consumer choice. *Marketing Science*, 4, 199–214.
20 Thaler (1985), see note 19.
21 Thaler, R. (1981) Some empirical evidence on dynamic inconsistency. *Economic Letters*, 46, 201–207.
22 Bar-Gill, O. (2004) Seduction by plastic. *Northwestern University Law Review*, 98, 1373.
23 Thaler, R. H. and Sunstein, C. R. (2008) *Nudge: Improving Decisions About Health, Wealth, and Happiness*. Yale University Press.

3

Consuming Statistical Data

Introduction

Much of the discussion in the previous chapter speculated about the mechanisms underlying psychological phenomena, asking under what conditions these mechanisms would be sensible. We tend to assume that the human mind is a rather sophisticated inference tool that has evolved over a long period, and that is probably not so bad at doing what it was designed to do. Indeed, for practically all modes of thinking we discussed, one can find good reasons and a variety of environments in which they are close to optimal.

This chapter is different. We will mostly discuss phenomena that are plain mistakes. Correspondingly, this is the least democratic of all chapters in the book: whereas in the others I keep asking you to make your own decision regarding what is rational for you, here I will use the authority bestowed upon me by the academic world to say, "Sorry, what you just said is wrong and what I say is right."

The reason might be that this chapter deals with statistical data, rather than with natural inputs. One can hardly make the case that the human mind has evolved to consume and understand statistical data, because such data are extremely recent in evolutionary terms. Some statistical techniques are about 100 years old, and yet they are

Making Better Decisions, by Itzhak Gilboa © 2011 John Wiley & Sons, Inc.

employed in innumerable studies, whose results are reported on a daily basis in the media. Thus, we are bombarded with statistical findings, and we try to analyze them using minds that have not changed since statistics was invented. It should not be a surprise that we need some help in this task.

This book is designed for people who have taken at least one introductory course in probability and statistics. Several statistical concepts that are taught in such a course are explained again in the context of the problems that follow, because, according to my experience, many students who have done well in a statistics course can still be quite confused about the meaning and applications of statistical concepts. As a result, very little prior knowledge is actually required to follow the discussion. If, however, you feel that you lack such knowledge, Appendix B may be of help.

Problems

Problem 3.1

A newly developed test for a rare disease has the following features: if you do not suffer from the disease, the probability that you test positive ("false positive") is 5%. However, if you do have the disease, the probability that the test fails to show it ("false negative") is 10%.

You took the test, and, unfortunately, you tested positive. The probability that you have the disease is:

Problem 3.2

You are going to play roulette. You first sit there and observe, and you notice that the last five times it came up "black." Would you bet on "red" or on "black"?

Problem 3.3

A study of students' grades in the United States showed that immigrants had, on average, a higher grade point average than US-born students. The conclusion was that Americans are not very smart, or at least do not work very hard, as compared with other nationalities.

What do you think?

Problem 3.4

In order to estimate the average number of children in a family, a researcher sampled children in a school, and asked them how many siblings they had. The answer, plus one, was averaged over all children in the sample to provide the desired estimate.

Is this a good estimate?

Problem 3.5

A contractor of small renovation projects submits bids and competes for contracts. He has noticed that he tends to lose money on the projects he runs. He has started wondering how he can be so systematically wrong in his estimates.

Can you explain that?

Problem 3.6

Comment on the following.

[At a restaurant] ANN: I hate it. It's just like I told you: they don't make an effort anymore.

BARBARA: They?

ANN: Just taste it. It's really bad food. Don't you remember how it was the first time we were here?

BARBARA: Well, maybe you're tired.

ANN: Do you like your dish?

BARBARA: Well, it isn't bad. Maybe not as good as last time, but…

ANN: You see? They first make an effort to impress and lure us, and then they think that we're anyway going to come back. No wonder that so many restaurants shut down after less than a year.

BARBARA: Well, I'm not sure that this restaurant is so new.

ANN: It isn't?

BARBARA: I don't think so. Jim mentioned it to me a long time ago, it's only us who didn't come here for so long.

ANN: So how did they know they should have impressed us the first time and how did they know it's our second time now? Do you think the waiter was telling the chef, "Two sirloins at no. 14, but don't worry about it, they're here for the second time"?

Problem 3.7

Studies show a high correlation between years of education and annual income. Thus, argued your teacher, it's good for you to study: the more you do, the more money you will make in the future.

Is this conclusion warranted?

Problem 3.8

In a recent study, it was found that people who did not smoke at all had more visits to their doctors than people who smoked a little bit.

One researcher claimed: "Apparently, smoking is just like consuming red wine – too much of it is dangerous, but a little bit is actually good for your health!"

Do you accept this conclusion?

Problem 3.9

Comment on the following.

CHARLES: I don't use a mobile phone anymore.

DANIEL: Really? Why?

CHARLES: Because it was found to be correlated with brain cancer.

DANIEL: Com'n, you can't be serious. I asked an expert and they said that the effect is so small that it's not worth thinking about.

CHARLES: As long as you have something to think with. Do as you please, but I'm not going to kill myself.

DANIEL: Fine, it's your decision. But I tell you, the effects that were found were insignificant.

CHARLES: Insignificant? They were significant at the 5% level!

Problem 3.10

Comment on the following.

MARY: My skin is killing me. Look how red it is.

PAULA: Yeah, it's really bad. Why don't you take something?

MARY: I tried everything. Nothing works.

PAULA: Nothing?

MARY: I'm telling you, I tried anything I could put my hands on.

PAULA: Look, maybe I can help you. I know this guy who works for BigMed, you know, the drug company.

MARY: Sure I know, they're big.

PAULA: Well, they are in the final phase of testing an ointment, and I think it's precisely for this type of rash. They need volunteers for the test – why don't you join the study? They even give you all kinds of skin products as a gift.

MARY: I don't need any gifts. If it can help, I have enough of an incentive to take it, believe me. But what if it's going to be worse?

PAULA: It won't. They're a serious company and the product has already passed many tests.

MARY: So was it approved by the FDA [Food and Drug Administration]?

PAULA: No, they're still testing it, that's the point of the test.

MARY: I don't get it. It's either/or: if you're so sure it's OK, why isn't it approved? If it's not yet approved, it's probably not yet OK.

PAULA: It's never 100% sure to be "OK," as you put it. A drug can be approved and then still kill people. It's all a matter of probabilities and statistics.

MARY: What does it help me that you call this probability? Again: either the probability is low enough so that it can be approved, or it's not low enough and then I don't want to take it.

PAULA: Which probability?

MARY: The probability that something bad might happen. I don't know what, but they are testing something, aren't they?

PAULA: It's up to you, of course. It's your skin and it's your decision. But we always take risks, when we board planes and when we play squash. All I'm saying is that, given BigMed's reputation, this is a very reasonable risk to take, and it's a pity to go on suffering.

MARY: Well, then, given BigMed's reputation, why are they still testing it instead of the FDA just approving it?

Conditional Probabilities

Problem 3.1 reads:

> A newly developed test for a rare disease has the following features: if you do not suffer from the disease, the probability that you test positive ("false positive") is 5%. However, if you do have the disease, the probability that the test fails to show it ("false negative") is 10%.
>
> You took the test, and, unfortunately, you tested positive. The probability that you have the disease is: _____

Many people tend to provide answers such as 95%, 90%, or something in between. The fact is that there is no way to tell. We will explain why in detail. In a nutshell, we are given conditional probabilities in one direction: of testing positive, and therefore also of testing negative, given having the disease and given not having it. But we are asked about the conditional probabilities in the other direction: of having the disease given testing positive. And we generally cannot figure out the conditional probabilities in one direction from the conditional probabilities in the other direction. What is missing is also some information on the unconditional probabilities, in this case the probability of having the disease a priori (unconditional on the test).

Let us first look at two extreme situations. Suppose that we take the test in a hospital ward in which all patients have already been diagnosed with the disease. Assume for simplicity that the previous diagnosis was done by many physicians and is beyond doubt. Now we apply the test to them. It is still true that the test has 10% of false negatives. That is, in the population of these sick patients, 10% will test negative. If I tested positive, what is the probability that I have the disease? The answer is 100%. It would have been the same answer if I had tested negative: because we anyway know that, being hospitalized in this ward, I have the disease, it doesn't matter what the test shows. That is, an unconditional (a priori) probability of 100% will translate to a conditional (a posteriori) probability of 100%.

Next assume that we consider a test for a disease that is long extinct. The test still has the conditional probabilities mentioned above – 5% false positives (within the population of the healthy) and 10% false negatives (within the population of the sick). These are properties of the test, its accuracy rates, which are independent of the population to which it is applied. But given that the disease is extinct, the unconditional, a priori probability that I have the disease is zero. After taking the test, it is still zero, no matter what the test shows. If the test happens to be positive, I'd simply shrug my shoulders and say, "Oh well, one of these false positives. We know they happen."

Thus, in the two extremes – where we *know* that the patient is healthy or that they are sick – the posterior probability, after taking the test, is precisely the same as the prior probability, before taking the test. The typical case will clearly be between these extremes, where the test does provide additional information. But these extremes tell us two things: first, despite the given conditional probabilities of testing positive (given being healthy and given being sick), the conditional probability of being sick given testing positive can be as low as 0% and as high as 100%. Second, an important piece of information that is missing for the calculation is the unconditional probability of having the disease.

To see the complete analysis, let us use some notation. Denote the two events in question by

D – having the disease
T – testing positive

and their complements, or negations, by

$\neg$ D – not having the disease
$\neg$ T – testing negative

We are given the following:

$$P(T \mid D) = 90\%$$

That is, the conditional probability of T (testing positive) given D (having the disease) is 90%. Since the conditional probabilities, given a certain event, also add up to 1, we know that the conditional probability of ¬T (testing negative) given the same D (having the disease) has to be 100−90%:

$$P(\neg T \mid D) = 10\%$$

Similarly, we are told that the conditional probability of T (testing positive) given ¬D (not having the disease) is 5%, or

$$P(T \mid \neg D) = 5\%$$

which implies

$$P(\neg T \mid \neg D) = 95\%$$

But what we are asked about is the conditional probability of having the disease given that one tested positive, that is

$$P(D \mid T) = \ ?$$

And it isn't any of the numbers given above. What is it, then? By definition, it is the ratio between the probability of both events occurring (the "intersection" of D and T) and the overall probability of event T. To compute it, it will be helpful to have a *probability tree*. This can be thought of as a decision tree in which you have no choices to make, and all the nodes are chance nodes. In such a tree conditional probabilities can be written on the edges:

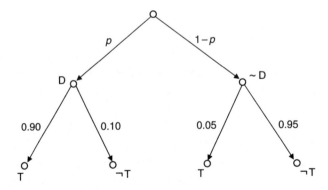

Decision tree 3.1.

With the aid of this tree we can compute the probabilities of the leaves, which are the intersections of two events. For instance, if we're interested in the probability of both having the disease (D) and testing positive (T), that is, the intersection of D and T, we can simply multiply the probability of D, p, by the conditional probability of T given D, 0.90. And the probability of D and ¬T will be the same p multiplied by 0.10. More generally, the probability of any leaf of the tree is obtained by multiplying all the (conditional) probabilities from the root of the tree to that leaf (see Appendix B):

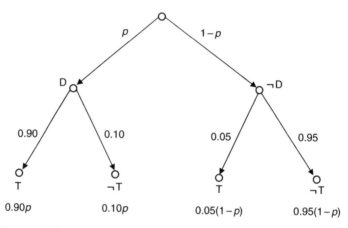

Decision tree 3.2.

What is the probability of disease given testing positive, that is, $P(D \mid T) = ?$ We need to take the probability of their intersection, and divide it by the probability of T. The tree above does give us the first: the probability of the intersection is $0.90p$. But what is the probability of T?

Here we have to work a little: the event T (testing positive) is not represented by any node in the tree above. But we do have two nodes representing disjoint events that together make up T: we have a node for T-and-D (T ∩ D) just mentioned above, and for its counterpart, T-and-(not-D) (T ∩ ¬D). The probability of T is, therefore,

$$P(T) = 0.90p + 0.05(1-p)$$

And we can now calculate the conditional probability of D given T:

$$P(D \mid T) = 0.90p \: / \: P(T) = 0.90p \: / \: \left[0.90p + 0.05(1-p)\right]$$

This formula reflects the points made above: (i) we can't tell what this probability is without knowing what p is, the unconditional probability of the disease ($p = P(D)$); (ii) as p varies between 0 and 1, so will $P(D \mid T)$. But besides these qualitative points, the formula also gives us a precise calculation of the conditional probability of having the disease *if we know the a priori, unconditional probability of the disease*. For example, if the disease is very rare, and has only 1% probability in the overall population, that is,

$$p = P(D) = 1\%$$

we obtain

$$
\begin{aligned}
P(D \mid T) &= 0.90p \: / \: \left[0.90p + 0.05(1-p)\right]\\
&= 0.90*0.01 \: / \: \left[0.90*0.01 + 0.05*0.99\right]\\
&= 0.009 \: / \: \left[0.009 + 0.0495\right]\\
&= 0.009 \: / \: 0.0585 \cong 0.1538
\end{aligned}
$$

To see that this indeed makes sense, it is sometimes useful to think in terms of frequencies rather than probabilities. That is, we imagine a large population, and translate probabilities to proportions. Assume, for example, that we have 10,000 people. With probability of disease $p = 1\%$ overall, 100 are sick and 9,900 are healthy. How many will test positive in each subpopulation? Well, this is what the conditional probabilities are telling us: the 10% of false negatives (among the sick) means that, out of the 100 sick people, 90 will indeed test positive, but 10 will walk home with the false reassurance that the test was negative in their case. As for the 9,900 healthy people, we know that 5% of them will test positive despite the fact

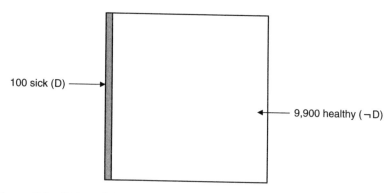

Figure 3.1   Sick and healthy people.

that they are healthy. That is, 495 (5%*9,900) will be healthy people who test positive, while the rest (95%*9,900 = 9,405) will be healthy people who are also told that they were found healthy on the test. Overall, those who test positive are 90 sick people and 495 healthy people, altogether 90 + 495 = 585. If I tested positive, I know that I am one of these 585 people. But I need not be one of the 90 sick ones – I may well be one of the 495 healthy ones who were false positives. What are the chances that I'm truly sick? Indeed, 90/585, which is about 15.38%.

Sometimes people find the sort of drawing shown in Figure 3.1 helpful. It is a sort of Venn diagram, where sets (or events) are represented by areas. It may be best to make the areas proportional to the sizes of sets (or the probabilities of the corresponding events). Sometimes, the diagram will only be schematic. For example, consider a square of 100 × 100 = 10,000 people, where the leftmost column represents the 1% of sick people (Figure 3.1).

Next, we split each of these populations according to those who test positive versus those who test negative (Figure 3.2). The conditional probability we were trying to compute, $P(D \mid T)$, is the size of the darker shaded area (90) divided by the sum of the sizes of both shaded areas (90 + 495 = 585), which yields 90/585.

An important lesson from this exercise is that it is quite possible that most sick people test positive, while most of those who test

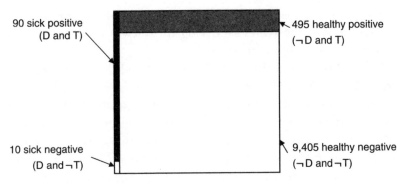

90 sick positive
(D and T)

495 healthy positive
(¬D and T)

10 sick negative
(D and ¬T)

9,405 healthy negative
(¬D and ¬T)

Figure 3.2 Positive and negative for sick and healthy people.

positive are not sick. Recall: the conditional probability of testing positive given that one is sick was

$$P(T \mid D) = 90\%$$

while the conditional probability of being sick given that one tested positive is only

$$P(D \mid T) \cong 15.38\%$$

More generally, the conditional probability of one event, A, given another, B, is quite different from the converse conditional probability, that of B given A. In particular, it may well be the case that

$$P(A \mid B) > 50\%$$

while

$$P(B \mid A) < 50\%$$

That is, it is possible that "most of the B's are A's" while "most of the A's are not B's." In fact, what relates the conditional probability of A given B to that of B given A is the ratio of the unconditional probabilities. Specifically,

$$P(A \mid B) = \left[P(A)/P(B) \right] * P(B \mid A)$$

(Throughout the discussion let us assume that all probabilities are positive, so that we won't be diving by zeros, and all conditional probabilities are well defined.)

Hence, if we are dealing with two events whose overall (unconditional) probability is the same ($P(A) = P(B)$ and $P(A)/P(B) = 1$), we will find that the conditional probability of the first given the second is the same as that of the second given the first. But this is not true in general. Yet, people tend to confuse the two conditional probabilities. Because this confusion is tantamount to ignoring the ratio $P(A)/P(B)$ in the formula above, Kahneman and Tversky referred to this phenomenon as *ignoring base rates*.[1] "Base" probabilities are the a priori, unconditional probabilities, $P(A)$ and $P(B)$. Ignoring them, or, to be precise, ignoring their ratio, is what results in the confusion of $P(A \mid B)$ with $P(B \mid A)$.

The phenomenon of ignoring base rates may have originated from the following fact: for any two events, if the first makes the second more likely, then the second makes the first more likely as well. Formally, for two events A and B, say that A *is correlated with* B if

$$P(B \mid A) > P(B)$$

that is, if knowing that A has occurred increases our belief that B will occur. You may recall that the overall probability of B is a weighted average of the conditional probability of B given A and the conditional probability of B given ¬A. (The weights are simply the probabilities of A and of ¬A – see Appendix B for details.) Hence, $P(B \mid A) > P(B)$ is equivalent to

$$P(B \mid A) > P(B \mid \neg A)$$

and to

$$P(B) > P(B \mid \neg A)$$

Reversing the roles, we can say that B is correlated with A if any one (hence, all) of the following is true:

$$P(A \mid B) > P(A)$$
$$P(A) > P(A \mid \neg B)$$
$$P(A \mid B) > P(A \mid \neg B)$$

The interesting fact, however, is that "being correlated with" is a symmetric relation: if A is correlated with B, then B is correlated with A. For example, suppose that you interview candidates for a job. Let A stand for "the candidate wears a business suit" and B for "the candidate is good." If it is true that, among the good candidates, you see a higher percentage of suit-wearing ones than you do in the entire population ($P(A \mid B) > P(A)$), then it is also true that, given that someone wears a suit, they are more likely to be a good candidate than if we knew nothing about what they wear ($P(B \mid A) > P(B)$). But we can't say anything quantitative. It is possible that most of the good candidates wear suits, while it may be far from true that most of the suit-wearing candidates are good.

The qualitative inference was true also in the example we started out with: the probability of testing positive was higher among the sick than among the healthy:

$$P(T \mid D) = 90\% > 5\% = P(T \mid \neg D)$$

(and this also means $P(T \mid D) > P(T) > P(T \mid \neg D)$ even if we don't know what $P(T)$ is). This implies also that

$$P(D \mid T) > P(D) > P(D \mid \neg T)$$

that is, testing positive isn't good news: the probability of being sick knowing that we tested positive is higher than the probability of being sick not knowing anything ($P(D)$) or knowing that we tested negative ($P(D \mid \neg T)$). But this is all we can say: if D makes T more likely (than before knowing D), then T makes D more likely (than before knowing T). Any additional quantitative inference will be unwarranted.

Importantly, the mistake of ignoring base rates, which all of us are prone to, is also the engine that keeps many prejudices alive. To consider a benevolent example, assume that many of the top squash players are Pakistani. What we mean by this is that, among the top squash players, there is a disproportionate representation of Pakistanis:

$$P(\text{Pakistani} \mid \text{top\_player}) > P(\text{Pakistani})$$

where the number $P(\text{Pakistani})$ refers to the proportion of Pakistanis in the overall human population. Thus, knowing that one is a top player makes it more likely that one is Pakistani than before we had this piece of information. This does indeed mean that the converse direction of the correlation holds *qualitatively*: given that one is Pakistani, one is more likely to be a top player than if we knew nothing about one's nationality:

$$P(\text{top\_player} \mid \text{Pakistani}) > P(\text{top\_player})$$

However, even if most of the top players are Pakistanis,

$$P(\text{Pakistani} \mid \text{top\_player}) > 50\%$$

we *cannot* infer that most of the Pakistanis are top players:

$$P(\text{top\_player} \mid \text{Pakistani}) \;?\; 50\%$$

And if you replace "Pakistanis" and "top players" by other groups and other features, you may find that certain prejudices and social stigmas may be rooted in the all-too-natural but hardly justifiable phenomenon of ignoring base rates.

Gambler's Fallacy

Problem 3.2 reads:

> You are going to play roulette. You first sit there and observe, and you notice that the last five times it came up "black." Would you bet on "red" or on "black"?

Many people respond that they would now rather bet on "red." It is, in fact, very difficult to justify this answer. The reason is the following. We can make the plausible assumption that consecutive spins of the roulette wheel are identically and independently distributed (i.i.d.):[2] each time the wheel is spun, each outcome has the same probability of coming up, and whatever we know about past spins tells us nothing about future ones. If this is the case, then there is nothing to learn from past outcomes about future ones, and the fact that the roulette wheel came up "black" five times in a row shouldn't change your probability that it will next be "red" or "black." This would be the case if you knew for sure that the roulette wheel was fair, that is, that "black" and "red" had the same probability in each spin.

It is possible that you're not quite sure that the roulette wheel is fair. In this case, you may still assume that consecutive spins are i.i.d. in "reality." That is, there is a certain physical mechanism that governs the outcome of the experiment, and this mechanism does not change from one spin to another, irrespective of how many spins we've observed as well as of their outcomes. Thus, the spins will be i.i.d. *given* (conditional on) the mechanism. However, if we are not sure what the mechanism is, then for us, subjectively, the spins are not independent. This is indeed the case whenever we take a sample in order to learn something about the distribution: given the distribution, we assume that the observations are i.i.d., but for us, not knowing what the distribution is, they are not independent. The whole point of statistical inference is that we can learn something about the distribution, and thereby also about future observations, from past observations.

But if this is the case, and we're not sure that the roulette wheel is fair, having observed five times "black" should make us put more credence on the hypothesis that the roulette wheel is biased towards "black." To consider an extreme case, if you were to observe 1,000,000 "black" outcomes, the only reasonable prediction is "black" for the 1,000,001st.

To conclude, if you are certain that the roulette wheel is fair, past observations are immaterial. If you're not certain, you should learn from past observations, but bias your estimate towards the more frequent observations. In either case, "red" doesn't seem to be more likely as a result of a sequence of "black"s.

Yet, people do make this prediction, which Kahneman and Tversky called "the gambler's fallacy."[3] Where is it coming from? Most probably, from an over-interpretation of the law of large numbers (LLN). This law, dating back to Jacob Bernoulli in the early eighteenth century,[4] says that if you observe a long sequence of i.i.d. random variables, their average will, with very high probability, be very close to their (joint) expectation. Thus, if the roulette wheel is indeed fair, then, as the number of spins goes to infinity, the relative frequency of "red" and of "black" will converge to the same number (slightly lower than a half, because the zero, or zeros, are neither "red" nor "black"). Knowing this law, people seem to be thinking along the following lines: "So far the empirical frequency has been rather biased: I observed five 'black's and no 'red's. But I know that in the limit the two outcomes should have the same frequency. Hence, 'red' has to 'catch up.' It must be the case that there will be more 'red's than 'black's in the future."

This reasoning is intuitive, but wrong. As Kahneman and Tversky put it, deviations from the expected frequency "are not corrected, they are diluted." For example, suppose that we observed 100 "black"s, and consider the next 1,000,000 spins. Assume for simplicity that each outcome is either "black" or "red" with probability 50%. Then the expected number of "black"s at the end of the 1,000,100 spins is 500,100, and the expected number of "red"s is 500,000. It is not as if nature is sitting there and thinking "Uh-oh, I put too many 'black's there, I should fill up some 'red's before Bernoulli gets upset with me." Nature doesn't really care about the past spins. It will continue to generate the random spins, but, as Bernoulli showed, in the limit we will get a relative frequency of 50%–50%. The first 100 spins will never be taken into account, but they will become negligible as the number of spins goes to infinity.

The gambler's fallacy is an interesting bias because it follows from too much knowledge, not from too little. Someone who has never heard of the law of large numbers is unlikely to make the gambler's mistake.

Children, who will often be prone to the other biases we discussed, will probably predict "black" after many "black"s have been observed.

The gambler's fallacy is related to two other mistakes that people make in dealing with probabilities. The first has to do with the classification of similar outcomes. Assume that you fill up a lottery ticket where you need to select six numbers out of 50. You ask me which numbers to choose, and I suggest "1, 2, 3, 4, 5, 6." "Com'n," you say, "this is ridiculous. I don't need to be a decision theorist to know that this is very unlikely. What on earth is the probability that the numbers will come out to be precisely this sequence?!" "Well," I would counter, "if you believe that these guys are not cheating you, you should believe that any six-tuple of numbers has the same probability. If you find 1, 2, 3, 4, 5, 6 highly unlikely (and I agree that it is!), then you should find any other sequence, such as 2, 5, 17, 18, 23, 45, just as unlikely. It probably follows that you should not play this game in the first place…".

In fact, I can even give you a good reason to choose "1, 2, 3, 4, 5, 6" over "2, 5, 17, 18, 23, 45": while both are just as likely to be the correct six-tuple, if other people think like you do, then, conditional on winning, you will have fewer people to share the prize with. But then you may argue that there are these nuts out there who do crazy things, or people who listen to decision theorists, or whatever. We'll conclude that the optimal choice has to do with the game played among the gamblers, and game theory belongs in a different course.

The point of this example is that when there is an obvious pattern, or a simple way to describe the outcomes, we understand how unlikely it is. When there are no simple patterns, we tend to lump outcomes together and think that the outcome is more likely than it really is. Namely, we think of the particular outcome as if it had the probability of all the outcomes resembling it. Thus, "1, 2, 3, 4, 5, 6" is classified as "the wondrous unique case in which we obtained six consecutive numbers, starting with 1," whereas "2, 5, 17, 18, 23, 45" is registered in our minds as "a relatively evenly dispersed six-tuple, with one consecutive couple." Going back to our roulette example, the sequence "black, black, black, black, black, black" seems more exceptional than the sequence "black, black, black, black, black, red."

If "black" and "red" are equiprobable in each round, the two sequences have exactly the same probability. But the former is easily described in a class of its own, namely, "only black," whereas the latter might be lumped together with others, as in "only one red in six spins." It is true that observing one "red" in six spins is more likely than observing zero "red"s. But any particular sequence with one red has exactly the same probability as the sequence with no "red"s at all.

The second mistake that is related to the gambler's fallacy is the confounding of conditional with unconditional probabilities. An old joke (that only probability teachers find funny) suggests that, if you're concerned about there being a bomb on a plane you're going to board, you should bring one bomb with you. The reason is that passengers do not normally carry bombs with them, and the probability of *two* such bombs is really small. Students, who may not laugh at this joke, are expected to see that the probability that is "really small" is the a priori, unconditional probability of there being two bombs. By contrast, the conditional (a posteriori) probability of two bombs, *given* that you already carry one, is the same as the probability of one bomb being brought by someone else if you don't bring a bomb with you. Similarly, the unconditional, a priori probability of six "blacks" is very low. But the probability of a sixth "black" after five have been observed is equal to the probability of "black" in a single spin.

To consider another example, assume that you are interviewing candidates for several positions. You're about to interview a candidate who studied in school A, and you recall that the last two candidates from school A were fantastic. "Oh well," you say to yourself, "this one can't be that good. After all, the probability of three great candidates is truly small!"

This would be another example of confounding conditional with unconditional probabilities. The unconditional probability of three great candidates used to be very low indeed, but, conditioning on the first two, the probability of the third being great is like the probability of the first candidate being great. If at all, you should be learning something about the school, just as the gambler may learn that the roulette wheel is biased, and update the probability that the next candidate is good upwards.[5]

Having understood all this, it is useful to mention that people sometimes make the opposite type of mistake, where they "learn" too much while facing independent phenomena. Suppose that you're going on a trip, and, at the airport, you discover that your MP3 player doesn't work. Worse still, the airline couldn't find your reservation, and the coffee shop's espresso machine was broken. You start wondering whether it is worth taking the trip. "With my luck," you say, "nothing good will come out of it."

In this case the three calamities that befell you seem causally and statistically independent. Importantly, they seem to be completely unrelated to the success of your trip. Yet, people often think in terms of "this isn't my lucky day," or "the stars are against me." Such thoughts are very natural, and they can be rational under certain assumptions. For example, you may assume that the alignment of the stars determines a certain luck variable, and, conditional on this variable, your fate is determined. The interesting fact is that even people who are not willing to make these assumptions explicitly might still think along similar lines. We often believe we find certain causal relations where they do not really exist.[6]

Biased Samples

Problem 3.3 asks your opinion on:

> A study of students' grades in the United States showed that immigrants had, on average, a higher grade point average than US-born students. The conclusion was that Americans are not very smart, or at least do not work very hard, as compared with other nationalities.

The conclusion may or may not be true, but it is not warranted given the data. One obvious explanation for the data is that the people who choose to emigrate from their country do not constitute a representative sample of their nation. For example, it is possible that only people who tend to have a certain personality choose to emigrate – say, those who have the resolve and determination to do whatever it takes to better their life conditions. It is also possible that the

77

population of immigrants was selected based on talent: people who have received negative signals about their abilities may wisely decide not to undertake the challenge of starting from scratch in a new culture. According to this explanation, only those who are talented (as signaled by their success in school and on the job in their home country) choose to emigrate. And there are many other possible explanations. The main point of the example is that the very fact that someone chose and succeeded to emigrate may be correlated with talent or diligence, which are presumably the variables of interest. Hence, when we consider a population of immigrants, we observe a biased sample of the population from which it was selected.

Note that, based on these data, someone might say that a randomly selected immigrant student is likely to be more successful than a randomly selected non-immigrant. This conclusion may be right, as it focuses on the population of immigrants. The conclusion that is not warranted was the one that took the immigrant population to be representative of the home country population. Whether a sample is biased or not depends on the question you are interested in: a sample will be biased relative to some populations but not to others.

Examples of biased samples abound. The most famous is probably the "Literary Digest" poll before the US presidential election in 1936.[7] The poll predicted that Landon would beat Roosevelt, who actually won the election. One problem with the poll was its use of phone and car registration lists. Not everyone had cars and phones in 1936, and the rich were over-represented in the sample. Since the rich tended to vote Republican more than the poor, the sample had a larger proportion of Republican voters than did the overall population.

Often the bias in the sample is inherent to the sampling procedure. For example, when you take a poll people choose whether to respond or not. Those who decide to respond may not be representative of the target population: you may get an over-representation of people who feel strongly about the issues, in one direction or another. Typically, people who have more time will find it easier to respond to polls. This might suggest that the poll will have an over-representation of retired or unemployed people as compared with the population as a whole. If the people who don't wish to respond to the poll also don't bother to vote, your sample will be fine; but if they do find the time to vote, the sample will be biased. Finally, another source of bias in polling is the converse phenomenon: many people do respond to the poll, and argue, often honestly, that they intend to vote, but eventually fail to do so. Finding a sample that will be representative of the population of eligible voters who eventually exercise their right to vote is not an easy task.

Another example in which the bias is introduced by the sampling procedure itself is given in Problem 3.4. The story there was:

> In order to estimate the average number of children in a family, a researcher sampled children in a school, and asked them how many siblings they had. The answer, plus one, was averaged over all children in the sample to provide the desired estimate.

The problem with this procedure is that a family with more children has a higher probability of showing up in the sample. For example, a family who has five children, all studying in the same school, has five times as high a probability of being sampled as a family who has but one child. And a childless family will disappear from the sample completely.

The *winner's curse* is also related to biased sampling. The term refers to a phenomenon which is demonstrated by the following example. Suppose that the government sells an oil field via an auction. The oil field has a *common value*: whoever wins it will enjoy the same profits. (This is in contrast with private values, where each potential buyer has their own subjective valuation of the object, as often happens in the case of art works.) However, this common value is not known with certainty. Assume that each bidder consults with experts, gets an unbiased estimate of the value, and bids it (or a bit below it, to guarantee some profit). The "unbiased estimate" means that, in expectation, the estimates are accurate. That is, with many such independent estimates, one can expect that the average will converge to the true value. Yet, it has been observed that the winner of the auction ends up losing money – and this has been referred to as a "curse" befalling the winner. In fact, there is nothing mysterious about this curse; rather, it's a natural statistical phenomenon: while the average estimate may be close to the true value, a bid based on the average estimate is unlikely to win the auction. The winner will typically be one of those who had the highest estimates. And these tend to be overestimating the value. In other words, while the overall population of bids is a representative sample of the distribution of the unbiased estimate, the population of bids *that end up winning the auction* is a biased sample.

Problem 3.5 is another example of the winner's curse. It reads:

> A contractor of small renovation projects submits bids and competes for contracts. He has noticed that he tends to lose money on the projects he runs. He has started wondering how he can be so systematically wrong in his estimates.

As in the auction for an oil field, contractors who submit their offers for a job have to estimate the cost of performing it, and submit a proposal that will leave them some profit. We should expect proposals at a lower cost to have a higher chance of being selected. As a result, *given that one wins the job*, one is likely to be on the low side of the proposals, and probably also on the low side of the estimations. Therefore, even if one has an unbiased estimate of costs, one may end up losing money on average: the projects one gets are not a representative sample of the population of estimates.

Regression to the Mean

Consider the dialog in Problem 3.6. Ann is complaining about the quality of food at a restaurant that she and her friend are visiting for the second time. Her friend, Barbara, points out that the restaurant is not new, so this cannot be explained by the general phenomenon of restaurants deteriorating after their inauguration. Are they simply having bad luck?

The answer is that this "bad luck" is something that could be expected. The reason is *regression to the mean*: if you select something due to its extreme past performance (good or bad), you should expect that its future performance will be closer to the mean. The mechanism behind this statistical phenomenon is quite simple: when you observe the variable, say "performance," you typically see the cumulative effect of an inherent quality trait, and a transient noise, or "luck" component. When you sample the same variable again, you should expect the trait component to be there, but the transient one to be re-sampled. Hence, if you truly thought that a restaurant was great, it makes sense that some of your experience is due to the chef's talent and innovation, and some of it to the lucky draw that you had – from the raw materials that the restaurant had that day to your own mood. When you come back, you should still expect the chef to be talented; hence you should expect an above-average experience. But the transient features are unlikely to be repeated, so you should not be too surprised to see that you don't enjoy the second time as much as the first. And this statistical fact is independent of any psychological aspects such as the novelty of the first experience.

Regression to the mean is also a type of biased sample – rather than select a restaurant at random, where we can expect that the noise factor will be, on average, the same as last time, we select a restaurant that we truly liked, which typically means that we select a restaurant based on a lucky draw of the noise variable. In other words, restaurants that were particularly lucky in their past performance have a higher probability of being visited again, and, given that, they have a tendency to perform below the level that resulted in them being selected.

This phenomenon can be observed whenever we use the services of a professional whose performance has some component of luck. This will include stock market traders and fund managers, as well as politicians.

Correlation and Causation

Problem 3.7 reads:

> Studies show a high correlation between years of education and annual income. Thus, argued your teacher, it's good for you to study: the more you do, the more money you will make in the future.

Clearly, this is an instance in which correlation between two variables is taken to reflect a causal link. It is true that, generally speaking, when a variable X is a cause of Y (say, high X values cause high Y values), we should expect X and Y to be correlated in the statistical sense (as measured by covariances, correlation coefficients, etc.). But the converse is false. We often observe correlations that do not reflect causal relationships.

In this example, a high correlation between education and income may indeed be a result of a causal link, according to which people with more education are better equipped to deal with market conditions and therefore can make more money. But it is also compatible with a converse causal link, as would be the case where people who already make a lot of money can afford to buy more education for the sake of fun. This theory can be quite plausible if by "education" we refer, for example, to the study of ancient languages. It is also possible that education and income are causally related only through a third variable. For example, if you have rich parents they may be able to afford to give you more schooling, as well as a head start in your professional life. Thus, the parents' wealth is the joint cause both of your education and of your income, but the latter need not be directly related in a causal link.

Problem 3.8 is another example of correlation that does not imply causation. It reads:

> In a recent study, it was found that people who did not smoke at all had more visits to their doctors than people who smoked a little bit. One researcher claimed: "Apparently, smoking is just like consuming red wine – too much of it is dangerous, but a little bit is actually good for your health!"

In this case we're a bit suspicious of the presumed theory.[8] With enough data we may accept it, but we'd like to think of the data critically. In particular, one wonders whether the positive correlation between smoking and health might be due to the fact that some of the non-smokers are sick people who were ordered to quit smoking by their doctors. Specifically, assume that the population of non-smokers consists of two disjoint subpopulations: one of people who have never smoked and who are generally healthy; and the other of people who smoked heavily for many years and were instructed to quit smoking because their doctors found them in a very high risk group. By comparison, imagine that the population of those who smoke just a little have smoked at this level for many years, and this low level of smoking has not had any significant effect on their health. In this case, we may find that the non-smokers are less healthy than the occasional smokers. But this is not because not smoking at all is bad for one's health. Rather, causation goes the other way around: some of the non-smokers do not smoke because they are (already) sick.

There are many situations in which it is quite obvious which causal theory accounts for a given correlation. For instance, when I find that most people at the hospital are sick, I should not assume that hospitals are bad for your health. Rather, hospitalization is a result of sickness. But often the relationship is far from obvious, as in the example of education and income above.

To establish causation, one usually prefers controlled experiments. If you can assign people to different groups randomly, and control their conditions, so that the only difference is the presumed cause, you can then observe the results and see whether indeed changing the cause (alone) has the presumed effect. However, such experiments are often impractical or unethical. They may be impractical because they would require a long time (as in the case of education), or a whole society to be used as a participant in the experiment. And ethical issues will often be relevant, whether we discuss people's health, education, or other determinants of their well-being in the long run.

While there are sophisticated statistical techniques that can help us tell causation from mere correlation, they are somewhat limited. In particular, it is very difficult to identify the causes of unique events such as stock market crashes, wars, and the like. For our purposes here, it is a good idea to recall that correlation does not imply causation. People often infer causal relationships where these do not necessarily exist, and people sometimes invite others to make such inferences. A little bit of doubt seems healthy in this context.

Statistical Significance

The dialog in Problem 3.9 is not meant to convince you to ignore possible risks. But it is supposed to remind you what "statistical significance" means. Significance is a subtle concept that is used in hypotheses tests. It is the maximum probability with which you allow yourself to make a "Type I error." What this means is the following: You wish to state a claim, call it A. You define it as your alternative, often denoted H_1. As your "null hypothesis," denoted H_0, you define the negation of your desired conclusion, not-A. In this example, if you wish to argue that mobile phones cause cancer, you state as your null hypothesis the claim that they do not, namely, that there is no difference in the probability of cancer between the population of mobile phone users and the population of non-users. Then you design a test: you will take a sample, and you will determine under which conditions you will decide to "reject" H_0, thereby stating your conclusion A. Rejection of H_0 is considered to be a statement (that its negation, H_1, is the case), while failing to reject H_0 is not considered to be a proof that it is true (even if it is sometimes referred to as "accepting H_0").

Before taking the test you ask yourself to what extent you are willing to make a false statement (Type I error) versus not making a statement that would have been true (Type II error). There is typically a trade-off between these two errors, and by selecting a test that "rejects" more or less often you can increase or decrease the probabilities of these errors.

It is important to stress that we do not know what the probability of making these errors is. To be precise, we can make a Type I error only if H_0 is true (and we nevertheless reject it) and a Type II error only if H_0 is false (and we fail to reject it). Thus, there is no possible world in which we can commit both types of errors. And we do not have a probability regarding which possible world we're in. *Neither before nor after taking the test do we have a probability that H_0 is true (or false).*

So what are the probabilities we are discussing? These are only *conditional* probabilities. Given a possible world, which might be consistent either with H_0 or with H_1, but not with both, we can compute the conditional probability of rejecting H_0 (or of not rejecting it). The "probability of Type I error" is the maximum such conditional probability. It is as if we range over all the possible worlds consistent with H_0, calculate the probability of rejection for each, and take the worst case, that is, the maximum probability. This is the famous "significance level" of hypothesis testing (often denoted by α).

The significance level therefore has to do with the probability of making a statement while it is not true. It has nothing to do with the content of the statement itself. Thus, it is possible that the use of mobile phones increases the probability of brain tumors from 0.0000302 to 0.0000303. If this is the case, the hypothesis "the probability is no more than 0.0000302" will be rejected, with a large enough sample, at any significance level ($\alpha > 0$) you choose. Yet, it does not mean that this difference is "significant" in any sense of the word. Of course, these numbers are made up, and I chose them so that they were tiny, and even the relative increase (from 0.0000302 to 0.0000303) was tiny. And, to stress the obvious, I'm not trying to promote the use of mobile phones. But I would like you to recall precisely what "statistical significance" means and what it doesn't mean.

Bayesian and Classical Statistics

The dialog between Mary and Paula in Problem 3.10 raises an important question about the meaning of statistical significance in hypothesis testing, and, in fact, also about the meaning of "confidence" as used in confidence intervals. You may note that the terms "confidence" and "significance" were chosen so as not to say the word "probability." The reason is that they are not probability, and should not be confused with this notion. This calls for an explanation.

Confidence intervals and hypotheses tests are techniques of *classical statistics*. This is the most common approach to statistical inference problems, where we consider a collection of distributions, look at observations, and try to find out which of the distributions are more likely to be behind these data. For concreteness, assume that we have a Normally distributed random variable X with an unknown mean μ and, for simplicity, a known standard deviation of $\sigma = 1$. Thus we know everything that there is to know about X apart from its mean (expectation).

Classical statistics provides several techniques to deal with the statistical inference problem "What is μ?" One is *point estimation*, where you compute a single number, based on the data, and hope that it is not too far from the unknown parameter, μ. In the problem we discuss, various criteria for the selection of a point estimator lead to the average of the observations. Another technique is *interval estimation*, where you construct an interval of values, whose end points depend on the sample, and hope that the interval "covers" (contains) the unknown parameter. Such an interval is called a *confidence interval* at a level of confidence, say, 95%, if it covers the unknown parameter μ with probability 95%.

Did we just say "probability"? Yes, we did. So what was that business about "confidence is not probability"? Here comes the subtle point: *before* we take the sample, we can say that the interval we will construct, after the sample has been observed, will cover μ with probability 95%. For instance, if we take just one observation, $n = 1$, the single point in the sample, X, has probability of 95% not to be more than two standard deviations ($2\sigma = 2$) away from μ. In symbols:

$$\text{Prob}\left(|X - \mu| \leq 2\right) \cong 95\% \tag{3.1}$$

This is a probabilistic statement about the random variable X. It is not a probability statement about μ, as the latter is an unknown parameter, not a random variable. What's the difference? We don't know μ, do we? Well, we don't know what μ is, and, in fact, we won't know what it is even after we take the sample. But in classical statistics we do not think of μ as a random variable with a distribution, expectation, variance, and so forth. It is just a number. A number we happen not to know, but not a random variable. Hence (3.1) is a probability statement about the random variable X. Recall that, for any particular value of μ, we know the distribution of X (assumed here $N(\mu, 1)$), and therefore we can make probabilistic statements about X *given* μ.

The beauty of (3.1) is that it is a correct probabilistic statement (about X given μ) *no matter what μ is*. That is: for every possible value of μ there is a different probability model. In each of these models, X is distributed Normally with a standard deviation of 1. These models differ in the expectation of X, μ. But one of the nice properties of the family of Normal distributions is that the difference $X - \mu$, that is, the deviation from the mean, has the same distribution. This is why we can state that X will be more than two standard deviations away from μ with probability 95%, and we can make this statement without knowing what μ is!

However, (3.1) is a probability statement about X. Once we have taken the sample and observed, for example, $X = 4$, the story is over. We get the confidence interval of $[X-2, X + 2] = [2, 6]$, and we know that it was generated by a procedure that, a priori, *used to have* a probability 95% of covering μ. This does not mean that the particular interval $[2, 6]$ does indeed cover μ with this probability, or with any other probability. After we have taken the sample, there is no longer any probability to speak of. Either $[2, 6]$ covers μ or not, but that's it. In classical statistics μ is not a random variable, neither before nor after the sample has been taken. Therefore, we can't quantify the uncertainty about μ in a probabilistic way (according to classical statistics).

Another example might help. Suppose that I roll a die, and that Y is the outcome. A priori, it has a probability of $1/6$ to be each of the values 1, 2, 3, 4, 5, 6. In particular, I can write

$$\text{Prob}(Y = 4) = 1/6 \tag{3.2}$$

This is a correct probability statement about the random variable Y *before I take the sample*. After I take it, I can't plug the value of Y into this expression and expect to get something meaningful. Whether Y happened to be 4 or not, I'll get a silly statement (such as "Prob(4 = 4) = 1/6" or "Prob(3 = 4) = 1/6"). The probability statement is a statement about the random variable Y while it was still random, so to speak. Once it has been observed and there is no longer any randomness involved, there are no interesting probability statements to make, and we surely can't take the probability statements we used to have and plug into them the value of the random variable we observed.

Exactly the same logic applies to statement (3.1). It is a statement about the random variable X, comparable to statement (3.2) about the random variable Y. Both make sense before the random variable in question has been observed. Neither would make sense if we plug in the value observed. The only difference is that statement (3.1) is a general template, which applies to any specific value of μ. But plugging the value of X into (3.1) is the same type of conceptual mistake as plugging the value of Y into (3.2).

Classical statistics therefore does not allow us to discuss the unknown parameter μ probabilistically. And this applies to other unknown parameters, too. For example, while we assumed that we knew that $\sigma = 1$, it is more realistic to assume that we don't know σ. In this case we can only say that

$$\text{Prob}\left(\left|X - \mu\right| \leq 2\sigma\right) \cong 95\% \tag{3.3}$$

which may not be very helpful. Luckily, we can also estimate σ by the standard deviation in the sample (typically denoted by s), and some combination of X and s has a known distribution – the t (or "Student t") distribution. The trick is that a certain function of the sample (a *statistic*) has a known distribution, even though the parameters μ and σ are unknown. And similar logic applies to the statistics that are known to have distributions, such as χ^2 and F. These statistics can be computed based on the sample alone (they do not depend on the unknown parameters), and their distributions are known, despite the fact that some parameters aren't. The reason we need statements such as (3.1) and (3.3), which hold for *any* values of the unknown parameters, is precisely that we can't quantify over these parameters.

Hypothesis testing is a very different statistical technique. As opposed to confidence intervals, hypothesis tests are tailored for a specific question, rather than being a general-purpose estimation. But there is an important feature that is common to hypothesis testing and confidence intervals: they do not treat the unknown parameters as random variables. They are trying to say something about the unknown distribution without assuming that we have probabilities over the distributions.

Hence, the notion of "significance" in hypothesis testing is not probability. It is related to probabilities *given* the distributions. For instance, assume, again, that X is Normally distributed with expectation μ and standard deviation $\sigma = 1$. Suppose that we try to claim that μ is positive. We then test the negation, that is, the hypothesis that μ is *not* positive:

$$H_0 : \mu \leq 0$$

versus the alternative hypothesis,

$$H_1 : \mu > 0$$

and if we manage to reject H_0 it is as if we proved H_1.

The "test" will tell us when to reject H_0. For instance, still assuming that we have only one observation X $(n = 1)$, we can decide that the rejection condition be

$$X > 2$$

We then ask ourselves what is the probability that we make a "wrong" decision. But this probability can only be computed given a value of μ. If $\mu \leq 0$, that is, H_0 is true, a wrong decision would be to reject it, that is, to make a statement (H_1) when it is wrong. This is a Type I error. What is the probability of making this error? Well, it depends on μ. If $\mu > 0$ this probability is zero: in this case the statement $H_1 : \mu > 0$ is true, and it won't be an error to make it. (One could then make only a Type II error, that is, to fail to make the statement.) If, however, $\mu \leq 0$, the probability of a Type I error is simply the probability of rejecting H_0, which we decided to do if and only if $X > 2$. It follows that, for every $\mu \leq 0$, the probability of a Type I error is

$$\text{Prob}(X > 2)$$

We do not know what this probability is, because it depends on μ, and we neither know μ nor have a probability over the values of μ.

What we can say is only a bound: in our example, this probability is going to be largest when μ is largest. And the largest possible value consistent with H_0 is $\mu = 0$. So the "significance level" is the highest such probability, computed for $\mu = 0$:

$$\text{Prob}(X > 2 \mid \mu = 0) \cong 2.3\%$$

The important point for our discussion is that this is the probability of an event stated in terms of the random variable X, *given* a value of μ. It is not a probability about μ. Neither before nor after we take the sample do we have a probability about μ, or a probability that H_0 is true.

There is a different approach to statistics, called the Bayesian approach (after Thomas Bayes, who introduced the notion of Bayesian updating[9]). According to this approach, anything we do not know is subject to probabilistic quantification. For example, if μ is not known to us, we can still have subjective beliefs about it and treat it as if it were truly random. That is, the Bayesian approach accepts the framework according to which μ is a fixed parameter that "in reality" doesn't change. However, as opposed to the classical approach, it argues that a parameter that is not known is, as far as we are concerned, just like a random variable. And then we can have probabilistic beliefs about μ – and this also means that we have a joint distribution of X and μ, and we can observe X and update the probabilities about μ according to Bayes's rule.

The Bayesian approach to statistics is much simpler than the classical one from a conceptual viewpoint. Rather than dealing with concepts such as "confidence" and "significance," which are close to "probability" but aren't probability, the Bayesian approach has only one concept – probability. In principle, it is always subjective. If we know that the distribution of X given μ is $N(\mu, 1)$, then all of us will have subjective probabilities that agree on this fact. That is, if you take two Bayesian statisticians, their joint distributions for X and μ may disagree about the marginal distribution of μ, but they will agree on the conditional distribution of X given μ.

And with this approach the only reasonable thing to do is to use Bayesian updating.

If the Bayesian approach is conceptually so simple, you might wonder, why do most textbooks teach us the classical approach, with all these complicated concepts? The answer lies in our tolerance of subjective judgments. Let's go back to the dialog and the new drug that Mary contemplates using. The Food and Drug Administration (FDA) has not approved it yet. In order to approve it, the FDA will run various tests, using hypothesis testing methods. Why doesn't the FDA use a Bayesian approach? Because in order to do that it will have to introduce some subjective judgments. In particular, it will have to have an a priori (unconditional) probability that the drug is dangerous, and then update this probability based on the samples it takes, to result in an a posteriori (conditional) probability. If, for the sake of argument, the FDA were to start with zero probability that the drug is dangerous, then, whatever the results of the experiments it runs, the posterior probability that it is dangerous will also be zero. (No amount of information can make a zero probability event a positive probability event as a result of Bayesian updating.) If, on the other hand, the prior probability of the event is 1, so will be its posterior probability. Both of these represent very extreme prejudices. Between these prejudices there is a continuum of much more reasonable prior probabilities. But whatever prior probability we choose, it will have an effect on the conclusion. To be precise, for any two different probabilities we can imagine a data set that will "prove" that the drug is safe under one probability, but conclude that it isn't safe under the other probability.

This degree of subjectivity is not desirable. Who is going to determine the subjective probability of the FDA? Do we want the outcome of the study to depend on their biases? Surely not. The FDA is supposed to be a government agency that provides the public with objective information. Well, you may say, how objective can it be? Nothing is perfectly objective in life. There are always some assumptions we make, implicitly or explicitly, that affect our conclusions. True. But it doesn't mean we shouldn't try. And this is what classical statistics is doing: it *attempts* to be as objective as possible. And to this end it has to shun prior beliefs, which are inherently subjective, and get into the conceptually complicated territory of classical statistics.

However, how about Mary herself? She can try the drug if she wants to. Should she do this, or should she wait for the FDA approval? While this is obviously her decision, we could give her the following piece of advice: "Look, Mary, the FDA is testing hypotheses, excluding any possible subjective input. This is fine, this is their job. But for your own decision making, there is nothing wrong in using your subjective judgment as well. If you believe that BigMed would not risk its reputation by submitting a drug that's not safe, you can use this judgment, as well as the fact that BigMed has indeed submitted the drug, and draw your own conclusion from this, namely that the drug is probably safe."

As mentioned in the dialog, very few facts are certain in our lives. And the drug may be dangerous even if it has passed all the tests of BigMed. In fact, it can still be dangerous even if it is approved by the FDA. The point is not that Mary can be certain that the drug is safe; the point is that classical and Bayesian statistics are techniques that should be used for very different types of problems. When you wish to *make a point*, that is, to be able to state a conclusion that would be accepted as "objectively (statistically) proved," your tool is classical statistics. When you wish to *make a decision* that is the best decision for yourself, and you don't need to worry about convincing anyone else, Bayesian statistics would be the method of choice.

Most of the statistics textbooks teach you the classical approach. It is the right thing to use for making points. Classical statistics is the method that would be used, for example, to test whether your product is safe if, God forbid, you're being sued. It is what you have to apply if you need to convince a board of directors that your new idea is great. And it is the main workhorse of scientific discovery in all fields, from economics and marketing to biology, psychology, and even physics. But it is important to recall that this is not necessarily the best tool for your own decision making.

When confronted with statistical data, you should ask yourself what it is that you're trying to do: to make the best decision for yourself or to make a point that could be "proved" to others? Based on this you should select the statistical approach that best fits your needs.

Exercises

1. A home owner who has a mortgage and who is not going to default may miss a payment on a particular month with probability 2.8%. (One who defaults obviously misses the payment for sure.) If Mr A missed a payment, what is the probability that he is going to default?
   a. 2.8%
   b. 2.8% / [2.8% + 1]
   c. 1 / [2.8% + 1]
   d. Cannot be determined.
   e. Can be determined, but differs from (a)–(c).

   _____

   _____

   _____

2. A leading newspaper followed up on the inflation rate predictions given by several economists. It selected the five with the best record, and asked them to predict inflation in the current year. At the end of the year, it appeared they were not so successful. The journalist concluded that we must be living in a very tumultuous period, when even top experts cannot make good predictions. This conclusion is:
   a. Erroneous, and it reflects the journalist's anchoring bias.
   b. Reasonable, because the journalist can't tell the inflation rate either.

    c.   Erroneous, as this might be a case of regression to the mean.

    d.   Quite likely, though the journalist may still be exposed to an availability bias.

_____

_____

_____

3. "Most journalists I met were superficial. Next time I see someone superficial, I'm going to ask them if they are journalists." Which statement would you endorse?

    a.   It's not enough to know that most journalists are superficial – maybe most people are superficial anyway. One has to look at the comparison between superficial people among journalists and among non-journalists.

    b.   Even if most journalists are superficial, it doesn't mean that most superficial people are journalists.

    c.   Assuming that there are many more superficial people in the population than there are journalists, the percentage of superficial among the journalists must be larger than the percentage of journalists among the superficial.

    d.   All of the above.

    e.   None of the above.

_____

_____

_____

4. Suppose that fashion models tend to be stupid more than the rest of the population. In this case:

    a.   We can conclude that the fashion industry tends to hire stupid people for modeling.

b. We can conclude that the life of a model tends to dull the mind.

c. We can conclude that the fashion industry chooses its models according to some criteria that correlate negatively with intelligence.

d. All of the above (all are warranted conclusions).

e. None of the above.

5. Your friend has a car repair shop, specializing in transmission systems. You told him you're considering buying a car of make A, which is not very popular. His reaction was "Don't get near them – I fix their transmission all the time. In fact, they're 90% of my business!" What can you say based on your friend's experience?

a. That, if you buy a car of make A, you'll have 90% probability of transmission problems.

b. That, if you buy a car of make A, you'll be more likely to have transmission problems than not.

c. That, if you buy a car of make A, you'll be more likely to have transmission problems than if you buy a car of another make.

d. All of the above.

e. None of the above.

6. A certain genetic disease is recessive, which implies that a child might have it only if both parents are carriers of the disease. The probability of each person being a carrier is 2%. One of two

prospective parents took a test and was found to be a carrier. Before the second took the test, the doctor said: "Oh, don't worry: I have seen people who were carriers of the disease in my life, but I've never seen two parents being carriers!" Do you support the doctor's view?

_____

_____

_____

7. We wish to estimate the expectation μ of a random variable X. We ask two statisticians, one classical and the other Bayesian, to do the job. The difference between them will be that:
   a. The Bayesian one will have a guess about μ even before taking the sample.
   b. The Bayesian one will not take a sample at all.
   c. The classical one will generate a confidence interval, but will not truly think that it contains the parameter μ.
   d. The classical one will prefer counter-intuitive answers.
   e. All of the above.

_____

_____

_____

8. The difference between confidence intervals and hypothesis tests is that:
   a. The confidence level is a probability only a priori, before taking the sample, whereas significance is a probability also after the sample has been taken.
   b. Significance looks at the difference between values of the unknown parameters, and not just at the probabilities of Type I and Type II errors.

c. Confidence intervals are a general-purpose estimation technique, whereas each hypothesis test is tailored to a particular statement.

d. All of the above.

e. None of the above.

Notes

1 Kahneman, D. and Tversky, A. (1972) Subjective probability: a judgment of representativeness. *Cognitive Psychology*, 3, 430–454.

2 See Appendix B for definitions and brief explanations.

3 Tversky, A. and Kahneman, D. (1974) Judgment under uncertainty: heuristics and biases. *Science*, 185, 1124–1131.

4 Bernoulli, J. (1713) *Ars Conjectandi*.

5 If, however, you *choose* to interview candidates from this school based on the great experience you've had with it, you should expect a disappointment, as discussed below.

6 In the social domain, this is often explained by attribution theory of motivation. See Heider, F. (1958) *The Psychology of Interpersonal Relations*. John Wiley & Sons, Inc.

7 See Squire, P. (1988) Why the 1936 Literary Digest poll failed. *Public Opinion Quarterly*, 52, 125–133.

8 Sadly, even the red wine theory has recently been questioned.

9 Bayes, T. (1763) An essay towards solving a problem in the doctrine of chances. Communicated by Mr Price. *Philosophical Transactions of the Royal Society of London*, 53, 370–418.

4

Decisions under Risk

Introduction

People have been making conscious, deliberate decisions under uncertainty for at least as long as recorded history. The Bible tells us about Jacob who is about to meet his brother Esau, whom he fears for good reasons.[1] Jacob decided to divide his camp in two, saying, "If Esau come to the one company and smite it, then the other company which is left shall escape" (Genesis 32:8). Clearly, Jacob was reasoning about a problem of decision under uncertainty; he seemed to have been risk averse, preferring to save half of his camp for sure rather than bet on saving all of it; and he had an intuitive sense of diversification.

However, probability theory was not invented until the mid-seventeenth century, and even then it did not lead very directly to a theory of decision making under uncertainty. In 1738 Daniel Bernoulli introduced the "St Petersburg Paradox,"[2] showing that it is unlikely that people behave as if they were maximizing the expected value of bets. Instead, he argued, people have a utility function, and they behave as if what they were trying to do was to maximize the expectation of the *utility* they get from the bet. Thus,

Making Better Decisions, by Itzhak Gilboa © 2011 John Wiley & Sons, Inc.

expected utility theory was explicitly inaugurated in the early eighteenth century, but the theory then remained dormant for another two centuries. While economics was making impressive progress, decision theory did not quite exist until the middle of the twentieth century.

At that time, however, things changed rapidly. Economics became much more mathematical than it had been, and much of it aspired to base economic predictions on theories of individual behavior. Decision theory and game theory were established as interdisciplinary fields that underlie different social sciences, and that nowadays extend to enrich other domains as well, such as biology and computer science. The formidable theories that were developed during that period are likely to serve as insightful guidelines for the foreseeable future. Yet, the accuracy of these theories in predicting actual behavior was soon challenged. This chapter and the following one are designed to explain the main ideas of the classical theory of decision under uncertainty, as well as some of its main criticisms.

This chapter deals with decision under the situation of *risk*, that is, with known probabilities. Probabilities are known, and explicitly given to us when we play in a casino, or buy state lotteries. Probabilities are arguably also known in more real-life set-ups, as in the case of an insurance problem. But probabilities are typically neither explicitly given to us, nor necessarily "known" in any meaningful sense in most of the important problems that we face in real life. For this reason, this chapter should be viewed mostly as a preparation for the following one. First, we make the simplifying assumption that probabilities are given, and try to see what decision making modes make sense for us in such set-ups. Only then will we proceed to the more involved problem in which probabilities are not given, namely decision under *uncertainty*.[3]

Problems

In each of the following problems you are asked to choose between two lotteries. A "lottery" gives you certain monetary prizes with given probabilities.

For instance:

A: $0   0.5
   $1,000   0.5

A is a lottery that gives you $0 with probability 50%, and $1,000 otherwise.

A "sure" prize will be represented as a lottery with probability 1, say:

B: $500   1

B is a "lottery" that gives you $500 for sure.

Please denote your preferences between the lotteries by

A < B   or   A > B

(or A ~ B if you are indifferent between the two).

Problem 4.1

A: $0   0.5   B: $500   1
   $1,000   0.5

_____

_____

Problem 4.2

A: $0   0.2   B: $500   1
   $1,000   0.8

_____

_____

Problem 4.3

A: $2,000   0.5   B: $1,000 0.5
   $4,000   0.5 $5,000 0.5

_____

_____

Problem 4.4

A:	$2,000	0.5	B:	$1,000	0.4
	$4,000	0.5		$5,000	0.6

Problem 4.5

A:	$0	0.2	B:	$3,000	1
	$4,000	0.8			

Problem 4.6

A:	$0	0.2	B:	$400	0.6
	$400	0.6		$500	0.4
	$1,000	0.2			

Problem 4.7

A:	$0	0.1	B:	$400	0.5
	$400	0.5		$500	0.5
	$1,000	0.4			

Problem 4.8

A:	$2,000	0.2	B:	$1,000	0.2

$4,000	0.2	$5,000	0.2
$6,000	0.6	$6,000	0.6

Problem 4.9

A:	$2,000	0.2	B:	$1,000	0.16
	$4,000	0.2		$5,000	0.24
	$6,000	0.6		$6,000	0.6

Problem 4.10

A:	$0	0.8	B:	$0	0.75
	$4,000	0.2		$3,000	0.25

The Independence Axiom

Let us start by comparing your answers to Problems 4.1 and 4.6:

Problem 4.1

A:	$0	0.5	B:	$500	1
	$1,000	0.5			

Problem 4.6

A:	$0	0.2	B:	$400	0.6
	$400	0.6		$500	0.4
	$1,000	0.2			

What were your choices? Many people find that they make the same choice in the two: they prefer either A in both, or B in both. There is some logic in such a consistency: suppose that I tell you that, with probability of 60%, you're going to get $400, and otherwise, with probability of 40%, you'll have to choose among A or B in Problem 4.1. That is, there is first a nature move, which is independent of your choice, and depending on this move you may have the choices in 4.1, or no choice at all (with $400 for sure). What would be your choice?

It seems plausible that you'll choose as you did in 4.1. Let us explain why. We begin with a decision problem that is neither 4.1 nor 4.6 (though we will argue that it is similar to both). Assume that nature first decides whether, with probability 60%, you get $400 for sure, or, with probability 40%, you get to choose between the alternatives in 4.1. We can draw a decision tree as follows:

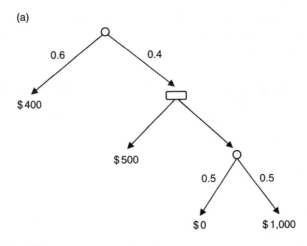

Decision tree 4.1a.

As in Chapter 2, a circle denotes a *nature move* or a *chance node*, that is, a random choice that is not up to you, and a rectangle denotes a node where you can make a choice. The numbers on the edges coming out of a circle (chance node) denote the probabilities with which you will find yourself in each possible branch, conditional on reaching the circle. In the first circle the probability numbers 0.6 and 0.4 are also the *unconditional* probabilities that nature would move left or right, respectively, because at the beginning of the tree there is nothing to condition on. At this level, with probability 0.6 you get the outcome $400 (for sure) and the game ends. With the complementary probability of 0.4 you get to the rectangle and you make your choice there. At the second circle the probabilities of (0.5, 0.5) denote the *conditional* probabilities of getting $0 and $1,000, given that we reach this circle (as a result of the first move of nature and of your own choice in the rectangle).

We don't have probabilities on the edges coming out of a rectangle node, because the probabilities are not part of the description of the problem – they are up to you to determine. In this example there is but one rectangle node: if you go left, you get $500 (for sure), and if you go right you get a 50%–50% lottery between $0 and $1,000.

The last chance node can be more concisely described also as a lottery, which is a list of pairs (outcome, probability). The last node above is the lottery that yields $0 with probability 50% and $1,000 with probability 50%, and we can write it as ($0, 0.5; $1,000, 0.5). Thus we can write the same decision tree as:

(b)

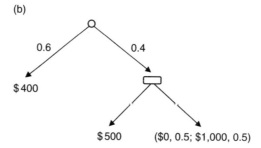

$400

$500   ($0, 0.5; $1,000, 0.5)

Decision tree 4.1b (concise representation).

Assume that you are asked to make a choice, before the game begins, as to your move at the rectangle node, if and when you get there. No one guarantees that nature will indeed move right and give you a chance to play. But if it does, you'll have to make a choice, and you're asked to determine what it is now (before knowing whether indeed you will have the chance to play).

What would you do? You may find the following reasoning quite convincing: "If nature moves left (at the first node) and I get the $400, it doesn't matter what I choose. So I should better focus on the second case. But here the problem is precisely that of 4.1! Hence, when asked, at the beginning, what would I do if I can play, I should choose as I did in Problem 4.1."

But if you accept this consequentialist reasoning, we may now ask you to look at the following tree:

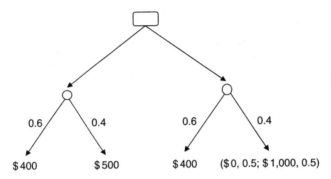

Decision tree 4.2.

Here you are asked to move first, and then nature moves. However, whatever you do, you have the same probability that nature will give you the $400 for sure (60%). And, whatever you do, you have 40% probability of nature moving right, where your choice does matter. Hence you may say to yourself, "It doesn't really matter whether I move first and nature second or vice versa. If nature gives me the $400 for sure, which will happen with probability 60% in either case, then my decision doesn't matter. And if nature goes right, my choice is the same as in the previous tree."

Observe that in Decision tree 4.2 you can imagine that nature's choice differs in the two cases. But since it has the same probabilities, and you never get to experience the two branches simultaneously, it seems like it shouldn't matter.

Finally, if you compute the overall probability of getting each outcome in Decision tree 4.2, depending on your choice, you find that these are exactly the choices of Problem 4.6: if you move left you get the lottery ($400, 0.6; $500, 0.4), and if you move right you get the lottery ($0, 0.2; $400, 0.6; $1,000, 0.2).

Taking all of these arguments together, we have a reason to make the same choice in 4.1 as in 4.6. While none of the arguments we used along the way is a logical necessity, they are all quite compelling: Problem 4.1 is described as a subtree of Decision tree 4.1; it seems logical to make the choice in this subtree as you would in Problem 4.1. (This is what consequentialism dictates here.) And if you make the decision before nature moves, there appears to be no reason to change your mind. (This is an implication of dynamic consistency.) But the choices in Decision trees 4.1 and 4.2 differ only in the order of moves, where, if you move first, you can't affect the choices made by nature. Finally, the overall distributions you choose between in Decision tree 4.2 are precisely those of Problem 4.6.

Let us move on. Compare your decisions in Problems 4.2 and 4.7. Again, they are related by the same reasoning:

Problem 4.2

A:	$0	0.2	B:	$500	1
	$1,000	0.8			

Problem 4.7

A:	$0	0.1	B:	$400	0.5
	$400	0.5		$500	0.5
	$1,000	0.4			

We may write

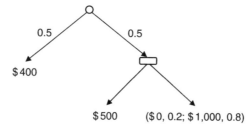

Decision tree 4.3.

and observe that the choice in the entire tree (made before the game begins) is equivalent to the choice in Problem 4.7, while the choice in the subtree that matters is precisely the choice in Problem 4.2.

Next consider Problems 4.3 and 4.8:

Problem 4.3

A:	$2,000	0.5	B:	$1,000	0.5
	$4,000	0.5		$5,000	0.5

Problem 4.8

A:	$2,000	0.2	B:	$1,000	0.2
	$4,000	0.2		$5,000	0.2
	$6,000	0.6		$6,000	0.6

If we "take out" the $6,000, we can write

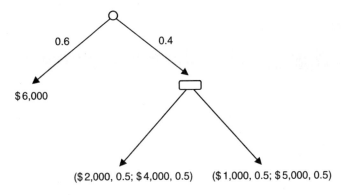

Decision tree 4.4.

Again, the same reasoning suggests that the choice in Problems 4.3 and 4.8 is the same. And on it goes: the same structure relates choices in Problems 4.4 and 4.9, and finally in Problems 4.5 and 4.10:

Problem 4.4

A:	$2,000	0.5	B:	$1,000	0.4
	$4,000	0.5		$5,000	0.6

Problem 4.9

A:	$2,000	0.2	B:	$1,000	0.16
	$4,000	0.2		$5,000	0.24
	$6,000	0.6		$6,000	0.6

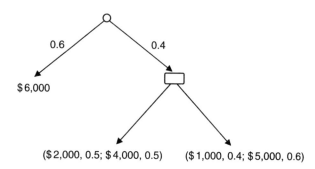

Decision tree 4.5.

Problem 4.5

| A: | $0 | 0.2 | B: | $3,000 | 1 |
| | $4,000 | 0.8 | | | |

Problem 4.10

| A: | $0 | 0.8 | B: | $0 | 0.75 |
| | $4,000 | 0.2 | | $3,000 | 0.25 |

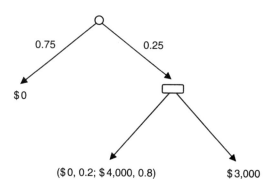

Decision tree 4.6.

In how many of the pairs did you indeed make the same decisions? A very common answer is that the first four pairs result in the same choice, but the last one doesn't. We'll discuss the last pair in the sequel. First, let us be more explicit about the underlying principle. Consider choices between pairs of lotteries, where each lottery, say, P, is a list of outcome–probability pairs as above. Consider two possible decision trees: in the first, you are simply asked to choose between two lotteries, P and Q:

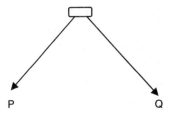

Decision tree I.

In the second, nature will first make a move. With probability $(1 - \alpha)$ you'll get lottery R, without any further choices on your part. With probability α, you can choose among P and Q.

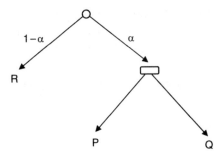

Decision tree II.

The *independence axiom* (formulated by John von Neumann and Oskar Morgenstern) suggests that your choices in Decision trees I and II should be the same, no matter what are the lotteries P, Q, and R. The answers to Problems 4.1–4.10 typically indicate that most people tend to behave in accordance with this axiom in many cases, but not all. Specifically, as mentioned above, it is common to observe choices that follow the axioms in the first four pairs but not in the last one. We will now see what this axiom implies, if indeed it is always followed.

Von Neumann and Morgenstern's Result

In 1944, John von Neumann and Oskar Morgenstern inaugurated game theory.[4] One of the by-products of their project was the following result. Suppose that a decision maker can compare any pair of lotteries. Assume that they do so in a transitive manner, that is, that if they find P at least as good as Q, and Q at least as good as R, then they also find P at least as good as R. Assume also that their preferences satisfy a more technical condition that is called "continuity." We won't get into its formulation here; I think it is fair to say that most people find it a reasonable condition once it's explained in detail. Finally, and most importantly, assume that the decision maker also satisfies the independence axiom stated above. Then, proved von Neumann and Morgenstern, the decision maker can be viewed as if they were maximizing the expectation of a utility function. That is: there exists an assignment of utility numbers to outcomes such that, for any pair of lotteries P and Q, the decision maker will always prefer the one that has a higher expected utility.

For example, assume that my utility function is

$u(\$0) = 0$
$u(\$400) = 0.5$
$u(\$500) = 0.6$
$u(\$1,000) = 1$

and you wish to predict my choice in Problems 4.1 and 4.6. Let's start with 4.1.

Problem 4.1

A: $0   0.5   B: $500   1
    $1,000   0.5

The expected utility of option A is

$$0.5 * u(\$0) + 0.5 * u(\$1,000) = 0.5 * 0 + 0.5 * 1 = 0.5$$

while the expected utility of option B is

$$1 * u(\$500) = 1 * 0.6 = 0.6$$

Hence, the expected utility of option B is higher than that of A, and if I satisfy von Neumann and Morgenstern's axioms, and I have the utility function above, I will prefer B to A.
  Next consider Problem 4.6.

Problem 4.6

A: $0   0.2   B: $400   0.6
    $400   0.6 $500   0.4
    $1,000   0.2

The same type of calculation would yield, for option A,

$$0.2 * u(\$0) + 0.6 * u(\$400) + 0.2 * u(\$1,000)$$
$$= 0.2 * 0 + 0.6 * 0.5 + 0.2 * 1 = 0.5$$

and, for option B,

$$0.6 * u(\$400) + 0.4 * u(\$500) = 0.6 * 0.5 + 0.4 * 0.6 = 0.54$$

Thus, option B has a higher expected utility. From the calculations above you may also see why someone who is an expected utility maximizer will satisfy the independence axiom: the common part to the two lotteries (above, $400 with probability 0.6) cancels out, while the remainder is proportional to the calculations we had in 4.1. The more interesting part of the result is the converse: someone who satisfies the independence axiom for any three lotteries

(P, Q, and R), and also satisfies the other axioms mentioned above, has to be an expected utility maximizer.

What does the theorem mean? Descriptively, it may convince us that there are more expected utility maximizers around us than we used to believe. If I were to ask you how many traders in the market can be assigned a utility function, such that their choices are predictable by maximization of the expectation of this utility function, you'd probably say, "not too many." Indeed, there are many traders who probably don't think in these terms at all. But the claim is not that the expected utility maximization necessarily describes the mental process that traders go through in their minds. Rather, it only says that this procedure may be a good description of their final choices (if we assume that traders face known probabilities). And if you now consider the independence axiom, and recall that maximizing expected utility is more or less equivalent to satisfying this axiom (and precisely equivalent to satisfying this axiom and the other ones), then you may believe that more traders can be so described. This is important since a lot of work in finance assumes that traders are indeed expected utility maximizers, and there have also been serious attempts to empirically estimate the utility function that characterizes traders.[5]

The theorem also has important normative implications: let's now forget about other traders, who may or may not be described by expected utility maximization, and ask what the best thing for you to do is. We agreed that you should be the judge of your own decisions. And the independence axiom may be one criterion to judge your choices by: after looking at some examples and explaining the independence axiom, I may ask you whether you would like to be the kind of person who satisfies it. That is, are you content with choices that violate it, or do you make the meta-choice of trying to make choices that are consistent with the axiom? If the answer is that you would like to satisfy the axiom, the theorem tells you something both important and useful: it tells you that the only way to satisfy the axiom is to behave as if you were out to maximize the expectation of a utility function. And there is a simple algorithm that guarantees that you'll satisfy the axiom: choose a utility function, and then always choose an option that has the highest expectation of this function. Moreover, any other algorithm that guarantees that you satisfy the axiom is equivalent to this one.

The next logical step is, therefore, to find out your own utility function, that is, the function that best describes your preferences (when used in the maximization of expected utility paradigm). Before we do that, we briefly mention that you need not always accept or always violate the axiom. After we complete the presentation of the classical theory, we will go back to Problems 4.5 and 4.10 and see why people may accept the axiom in most cases, but consciously choose to violate it in other cases. If these are your preferences, the expected utility idea, and the utility function we are about to measure, will only serve as first approximations of your preferred modes of decision making under risk.

Measurement of Utility

Let us now assume that you made your choice to maximize the expectation of *a* utility function, and all that's left for you to determine is which function suits you best. Here a nice surprise awaits you: you only need to determine your preferences between lotteries that have three different outcomes. In fact, if you can compare any pair of lotteries, where you have two possible outcomes in one and a single possible outcome in the other, you will be able to pinpoint your utility function precisely. This means that if you know what your preferences are in these simple situations, you will know your utility function, and will find the only way to make decisions consistent with this function in more complicated situations.

Consider the example shown in Table 4.1. You have to choose between two lotteries, P and Q.

The choice between P and Q may be quite confusing. P seems to be less risky. It promises at least $200, while Q may yield nothing. But Q has a much higher probability of getting $1,000. What should you do?

Table 4.1 Two lotteries P and Q.

Outcome in $, x	Probability under P, P(x)	Probability under Q, Q(x)
0	0	0.10
200	0.10	0.20
400	0.20	0.20
600	0.40	0.05
800	0.20	0.15
1,000	0.10	0.30

The idea of measuring, or calibrating, your utility function would work as follows. The function will be unique only up to changes in the unit of measurement and shifts of zero. That is, we have two degrees of freedom when we select the particular function, similar to the freedom we have in measuring temperature. When we switch from a Fahrenheit to a Celsius scale we perform a linear transformation, multiplying by a positive constant and adding (or subtracting) a constant. Precisely the same freedom will be allowed here. Put differently, we can choose which outcome will get a utility of zero and which a utility of 1 (provided that the latter is better than the former), and the rest will be determined uniquely.

Let us simplify matters by setting the worst outcome to 0 and the best to 1:

$$u(0) = 0$$
$$u(\$1,000) = 1$$

Let us now try to figure out what is the utility of $200. Suspecting the function might be linear in money, we may start by asking which of the following options you prefer:

A: $0 0.8   B: $200 1
    $1,000 0.2

The expected utility of option A is

$$0.8 * u(\$0) + 0.2 * u(\$1,000) = 0.8 * 0 + 0.2 * 1 = 0.2$$

while that of B is

$$1 * u(\$200) = u(\$200)$$

If you happen to be indifferent between A and B, it must be the case that

$$u(\$200) = 0.2$$

In this case we're lucky and our job is done: we found the unique value of u($200) that describes your preferences in the decision problem above, and this value will have to serve in all future calculations of expected utility involving the outcome $200. If we were not that lucky, we distinguish between two cases: if you prefer A to B we conclude that

$$u(\$200) < 0.2$$

while if you prefer B to A we conclude that

$$u(\$200) > 0.2$$

Whatever the answer, we can continue by changing the probability of getting $1,000 in A, and finding the probability that would yield indifference. For instance, if you prefer B to A, we may ask you to compare

A':	$0	0.7	B:	$200	1
	$1,000	0.3			

Basically asking whether u($200) is larger or smaller than 0.3, and so on. Finally, we will find a value p such that you are indifferent between

A':	$0	1−p	B:	$200	1
	$1,000	p			

And it follows that u($200) = p.

Continuing in this way for the other outcomes, $400, $600, and $800, we find their utility values. Each time we only make very simple comparisons – the sure outcome on the one hand, and a lottery between two outcomes on the other. These simple questions suffice to uniquely determine the utility function, and they give you a powerful tool in assessing the utility function you would like to use, if indeed this idea appeals to you.

Risk Aversion

Let us go back to Problem 4.1. You were asked to compare a lottery (A) with a sure outcome (B). In this case, the sure outcome happened to be exactly the expected value of the lottery:

$$0.5 * \$0 + 0.5 * \$1,000 = \$500$$

Does it mean that you have to be indifferent between the two? The answer is negative. Expectation is but one way to summarize a whole distribution of a numerical random variable by a single number. There are other numbers that tell us something about the random variable, such as the median and the mode. Further, we can also compute the random variable's standard deviation in an attempt to measure its dispersion, or, in a case of a lottery, riskiness. Indeed, option A is a lottery with a positive standard deviation, while option B has a standard deviation of zero. Thus, there is nothing in probability theory that tells us that we have to choose the random variable with the highest expected value. If we were facing a repeated decision, under the same conditions, where the random variables were independent, we would know that the expectation means quite a bit due to the law of large numbers: in this case, the average of many random variables would be very close to the expectation, with very high probability. But in a one-short decision problem as above, the expectation need not mean that much.

In contrast to the expected value of the random variable, the expected *utility* means more. As discussed above, von Neumann–Morgenstern's theorem states that very mild assumptions imply that you would want to behave as if you were maximizing the expectation of a certain utility function. This theorem does not tell you which utility function to choose; it only says that there exists one that describes your tastes. If your utility function is linear in money, that is, if

$$u(\$x) = a * x + b$$

for some parameters, $a > 0$, and b, we can also assume that

$$u(\$x) = x$$

(because the von Neumann–Morgenstern utility is anyway given up to a linear transformation, so that we can simply set $a = 1$ and $b = 0$). In this case, an expected utility maximizer will also be an *expected value maximizer*, that is, he will choose the lottery with the higher expectation. But many decision makers do not behave in this way. In particular, if you prefer B to A in Problem 4.1, your von Neumann–Morgenstern utility function (assuming you have one) cannot be linear.

A decision maker who always prefers the expected value of a lottery (such as B) to the lottery itself (such as A) is called *risk averse*. It turns out that, if the decision maker maximizes the expected value of a von Neumann–Morgenstern function, u, risk aversion is equivalent to the utility function being *concave*. This means that the graph of the function is always above each of its strings. More concretely, take any two sums of money, x and y. Consider the straight line segment that connects the points on the graph, $(x, u(x)),(y, u(y))$. The function is (strictly) concave if, in between x and y, the graph of the function is (strictly) above the segment connecting the two (see Figure 4.1).

To see why concavity of the function u relates to risk aversion, consider a simple case as in Problem 4.1. Suppose that your wealth level is W and that I offer you a bet of \$100 on a fair coin. Thus, with probability of 50% you'll gain \$100, and will have $W + 100$, and with probability of 50% you'll lose \$100, and will have $W - 100$. You may think of your gain as a random variable, X, with the following distribution:

$$X = \begin{cases} +100 & 0.50 \\ -100 & 0.50 \end{cases}$$

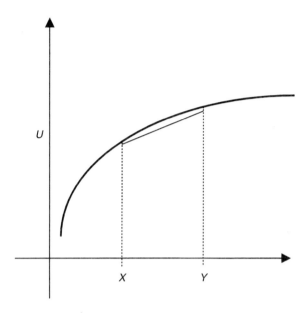

Figure 4.1   A concave function.

If you take the bet, you will have a wealth of $W + X$, that is, the random variable

$$W + X = \begin{cases} W + 100 & 0.50 \\ W - 100 & 0.50 \end{cases}$$

And if you refuse the bet, you are left with your wealth, W, for sure. Assuming that you maximize the expectation of a function $u(x)$, what will be your decision?

Consider the graph shown in Figure 4.2. If you refuse the bet, you are left with W for sure, and the utility is $u(W)$ with probability 1, implying that the expected utility is $u(W)$.

If you take the bet, you get the risky variable $W + X$, which can take the values $W + 100$ and $W - 100$ with equal probability. Hence the utility of your wealth will be $u(W + 100)$ with probability 50%, and $u(W-100)$ with probability 50%. Thus, the expected utility is

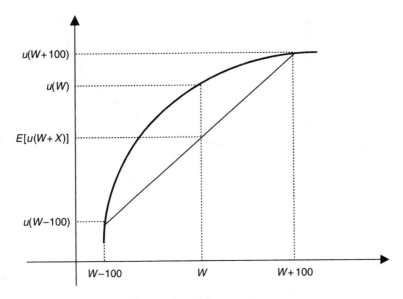

Figure 4.2 Concavity of *u* implies risk aversion.

$$E\big[u(W+ X)\big]=0.5*u(W+100)+0.5*u(W-100)$$

This is the point, on the vertical axis, that is half way between $u(W + 100)$ and $u(W-100)$. It corresponds to the point W on the string. That is, the point $(W, E[u(W + X)])$ is precisely the mid-point of the segment connecting $(W-100, u(W-100))$ and $(W + 100, u(W + 100))$. As the graph shows, if the function *u* is concave, the value *u(W)* is above $E[u(W + X)]$. That is, the utility of the expectation of $W + X$ is higher than the expectation of the utility of that random variable. You can also imagine why this would be true if the probabilities involved were not 50%–50%, or if the gain and the loss were not equal. Graphically, the line segment describes the expected utility of the bet (which is a linear combination of the utility values at the extremes), while the graph of the function describes the utility of the expected value. In fact, this will be true of any random variable, not only one that takes only two values: the function *u* is concave *if and only if*, for every random variable, the expectation of the utility is

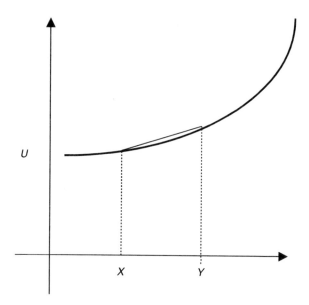

Figure 4.3 A convex function.

lower than the utility of the expectation (with the possibility of equality in degenerate cases, where there is no risk involved).[6]

You may imagine that one can also exhibit *risk loving* (or *risk seeking*) behavior. This would mean that the decision maker prefers the random variable to its expectation (with certainty). For expected utility maximizers, this behavior is equivalent to a *convex* utility function, that is, a function that is always *below* its strings (see Figure 4.3).

Risk aversion is typically assumed in economics and finance. Indeed, when we buy insurance, we probably exhibit risk aversion: the premium is higher than the expected loss. How do we know that? Because the insurance company does not insure a single client – it insures many of them, who are more or less independent, and presumably also similar in terms of the risk they face. Thus, the insurance company faces many random variables that are roughly i.i.d. (independently and identically distributed), and it may rely on the law of large numbers to calculate its average loss with very high accuracy (and very high probability). If the insurance company were to price the premium below the expected loss, it would lose money. Hence we can assume that, at least in most cases, insurance companies price premiums above the expected losses. Why do we, as individuals, still purchase the insurance? Because, facing a single random variable, the expected value is not so meaningful to us. And if we are risk averse, we will be willing to pay the insurance company to take the burden of risk off our shoulders. But this explanation does presume that the insurance company's clients are risk averse. Risk loving clients would not buy policies that are more expensive than the expected loss. By this logic, anyone who buys insurance behaves, at least in this problem, in a risk averse manner.

Gambling in casinos is typically given as the converse example: if I gamble in a casino, I walk in with a given, certain, amount of money, and pay something to play a game that gives me a random payoff in return. This would make a lot of sense if the expected payoff were higher than the cost of playing. In this case, you could think of me as investing: putting money into an uncertain prospect, but one that has a sufficiently high probability of yielding sufficiently high profits to result in a positive expectation. However, we don't really believe that the casino is offering us gambles with positive expected gains. The reason is, again, the law of large numbers: if the casino were to offer such a gamble, since it offers identical gambles to many independent clients, it would lose money. Indeed, casino games have well-defined probabilities, and we can compute and find out that they offer a negative expected payoff. (An exception is Black Jack, where, I've been told, you can obtain a positive expected payoff if you manage to count and recall which cards have been drawn.)

Clearly, the same logic applies to state lotteries: you may verify that the expected gain is lower than the cost of participation. Indeed, the state makes money due to the law of large numbers. It would appear that only risk loving people would buy state lotteries, just as only risk averse people would buy insurance policies. But then what do we do with people who simultaneously buy insurance (say, against losing their houses) and lottery tickets? Are they risk averse or risk loving?

There is a possibility of explaining such a behavior by maximization of expected utility with a function that is neither (everywhere)

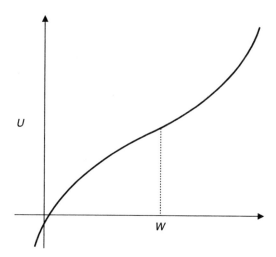

Figure 4.4 A graph of a function that is concave in part of the range and convex in another.

convex nor (everywhere) concave: if it were concave when it came to low payoffs, and convex when it came to high ones, you could explain such a behavior (see Figure 4.4).

With such a function, starting at wealth level *W*, when I look upwards towards the potential gains promised by the lottery (or the casino), I behave in a risk loving way, preferring the bet over the sure expected value; but when I look downwards towards the possible losses, involving the loss of my property, I behave in a risk averse way, and buy insurance.

This explanation is a little problematic, since it requires that *all* the individuals who simultaneously buy insurance and lottery tickets be around the inflection point of their utility function. Were such individuals to gain a lot of money, they would find themselves in the convex range of the function, and stop buying insurance. But we do find rich people insuring their properties, and poor people tend to buy lottery tickets more than the rich. It actually seems more reasonable that the inflection point "moves around" with the wealth level – but this means that we don't have a utility function that is defined on the bottom-line levels of wealth, but on changes in wealth, that is, wealth compared with the level we already have. This idea will lead us to an important contribution of prospect theory, to be discussed shortly. However, it is not obvious that gambling behavior should fit into the mold of expected utility theory with monetary payoffs. It seems more reasonable that a large part of the payoff to gamblers is the excitement, the time they spend waiting for the lottery's outcome, fantasizing about what they would do with their gains, or praying to Lady Luck. None of these non-monetary payoffs are captured in the "outcomes" of the lotteries above, and it's not clear that we should try to capture them by the curvature of the utility function.

Economic and finance theory go on to specify particular functional forms of the utility functions that characterize economic agents, investors, and so on. There are ways to measure risk aversion, in absolute terms as well as in relative terms, as a proportion of current wealth. The functional forms that give rise to constant absolute risk aversion and constant relative risk aversion have been very popular in theoretical and empirical studies. They are, however, beyond the scope of this book.

Prospect Theory

Let us go back to the independence axiom. You may recall that we had five pairs of choices that were related by this axiom: the axiom requires that you make the same decision in Problem 4.1 as in Problem 4.6, in Problem 4.2 as in Problem 4.7, and so on. We mentioned that it is quite common to observe decision makers following the axiom in the first four pairs but not in the last one. This one was:

Problem 4.5

A:	$0	0.2	B:	$3,000	1
	$4,000	0.8			

Problem 4.10

A:	$0	0.8	B:	$0	0.75
	$4,000	0.2		$3,000	0.25

Many people choose B in 4.5 but A in 4.10. Moreover, even when the independence axiom is explained in this context, many people insist that, while they see the logic of the axiom, they would not like to follow it in this example. Asked for the reason, people often say that in 4.5 option B offers them certainty.

This example was suggested by Kahneman and Tversky,[7] based on an example of Maurice Allais (dating back to the 1950s).[8] They argued that the example illustrates the "certainty effect," namely the "extra bonus" that certainty yields.

Consider another example of the same type, but this time with no certainty involved:

Problem 4.11

A:	$0	0.2	B:	$0	0.6
	$1,000,000	0.8		$2,000,000	0.4

Problem 4.12

A:	$0	0.9992	B:	$0	0.9996
	$1,000,000	0.0008		$2,000,000	0.0004

A typical pattern of preferences here would rank A over B in 4.11 but B over A in 4.12. This, again, is a violation of the independence axiom. You can verify that the probabilities of getting the positive payoffs in both lotteries in 4.12 are the same as in 4.11, only divided by 1,000. The ratio of the probabilities (of getting 1 million dollars in A to that of getting 2 million dollars in B) is the same across the two problems. The independence axiom would have implied that the same choice be made in these problems. In fact, if you "mix" the lotteries in 4.11 with zero, attaching probability 0.999 to zero and 0.001 to the lotteries, you get the respective lotteries in 4.12. But in Problem 4.11 people often say, "Hey, I prefer to have a probability of 80% of being a millionaire rather than a probability of 40%, even if I do get more money in the latter case." By contrast, the probabilities of getting the money in Problem 4.12 seem so small that people tend to ignore them. Kahneman and Tversky referred to this phenomenon

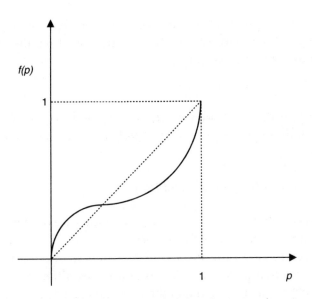

f(p)

Figure 4.5 A typical graph of the probability distortion function.

as "the common ratio effect." In fact, the different choices in Problems 4.5 and 4.10 can also be explained by the common ratio effect.

In a famous article bearing this title, Kahneman and Tversky offered "prospect theory"[9] as an alternative to expected utility theory for decision making under risk. One aspect of the theory was the claim that people react to stated probabilities in a non-linear way. It is as if decision makers were distorting the probabilities they were faced with: the *decision weights* implicitly assigned to given payoffs in actual behavior do not depend on the probability in a linear way. Specifically, assume that the decision maker has a function f that looks as in Figure 4.5. The function is strictly increasing, taking the value 0 at $p = 0$ and the value 1 at $p = 1$. It is assumed to be above the 45° line for small probabilities, and below it for large ones. Thus, small probabilities are magnified in the decision making process, and very large ones (close to 1) are treated as if they were smaller than they really are.

Let us assume that we are given the prospect of gaining x_i dollars with probability p_i, for $i = 1, \ldots, n$, where the sum of all p_i's is 1. (The use of the word "prospect" will be explained shortly.) Von Neumann–Morgenstern expected utility theory suggests that the decision maker maximizes the formula

$$p_1 u(x_1) + p_2 u(x_2) + \ldots + p_n u(x_n)$$

for an appropriately chosen function u. By contrast, one version of prospect theory[10,11] suggests that the decision maker chooses a maximizer of

$$f(p_1) u(x_1) + f(p_2) u(x_2) + \ldots + f(p_n) u(x_n)$$

You can verify that violations of the independence axiom mentioned above can be explained by this theory.

However, prospect theory has another, no less important ingredient: it claims that people treat gains and losses differently. To draw this distinction, it supposed that the decision maker has a certain *reference point* with which payoffs are compared. Payoffs that are higher than the reference point are perceived as gains, and payoffs that are lower than the reference point as losses. Kahneman and Tversky argued that people react differently to gains versus losses. In particular, people are averse to losses. This *loss aversion* goes beyond the obvious fact that people prefer more money to less. It suggests that a given amount of money, if perceived as a loss relative to the reference point, will be considered a more painful outcome than the same amount when perceived as a gain. Importantly, prospect theory holds that people react to *changes* rather than to *absolute levels*. Kahneman and Tversky used the term *value function* for the function that governs behavior under risk. The change of term from *utility* to *value* should remind us that the function has a different interpretation than in expected utility theory: it is still defined on real numbers, denoting sums of money, but these numbers are changes from the reference point, rather than the bottom-line levels of wealth.

The ideas of a reference point and the *gain–loss asymmetry* that Kahneman and Tversky postulated, as well as the notion of reaction to changes rather than to absolute levels, are related to other phenomena in psychology. Adaptation level theory (developed by Harry

Helson in 1947)[12] suggests that most of our perceptions adapt to given levels of stimuli. The pupils of our eyes enlarge and contract to adjust to the level of light; we get used to odors and background noises, and so forth. The logic behind these phenomena is that our minds react to changes, which typically carry new information, and tend to ignore constant stimuli, which do not offer meaningful new data. This does not mean that we adjust to anything and everything; indeed, if I hold my hand by the fire, I will not say, "Oh well, fire, sure, I already know that there is fire out there." Rather, I will feel scorching that becomes more painful as I keep my hand by the fire, until I pull it away. Generally, when there is a clear and immediate danger, no adaptation will take place, as action is needed. But if, for instance, it gets dark towards the evening, there is nothing I can do to change it, and there is no immediate danger in darkness per se. Hence it makes sense to adapt to the lower level of light by enlarging my pupils. More generally, apart from cases of severe danger, it makes sense to react to changes rather than to absolute levels of the stimuli around us.

In 1955, Herbert Simon offered the theory of *bounded rationality*. He suggested that people do not optimize; rather, he argued, they *satisfice*.[13] What that means is the following: people walk around with a certain *aspiration level* for their performance in their minds. As long as their performance is above that level, they are *satisficed* and they keep doing whatever they have been doing. When they notice that their performance is below that level, they get into action and try to see what can be done differently; they start experimenting with other options, and so on. In particular, Simon was modeling managers, who have too many decisions to make, often with too little information. They can't possibly study each and every problem in detail, and thus, as long as things are OK, they don't change them. But they do make sure they put out fires when these erupt.

The reference point of Kahneman and Tversky is a new idea, which differs both from the aspiration level of Simon and from the adaptation level of Helson. But these other ideas indicate that various theories in psychology concur that human beings do not respond only to absolute levels, and that, in particular, a certain point on the payoff scale may play a special role.

You may recall Problem 2.2 and Problem 2.13 from the beginning of this book, which also had a flavor of gain–loss asymmetry. In these problems, the same gains (of $1,000, $1,500, and $2,000) were presented once as gains (relative to $1,000) and once as losses (relative to $2,000), typically resulting in different behavior. While these were also examples of framing effects, they hinged on the gain–loss asymmetry documented by Kahneman and Tversky, and, in particular, on loss aversion. Generally, Kahneman and Tversky argued that the prevalent phenomenon of risk aversion is typical of the range of gains, but not of losses. In fact, they found that in the realm of losses people are often risk loving, and that their value function in this domain tends to be convex rather than concave. Their explanation of this phenomenon was not that people truly enjoy the risk, but that they dislike losing so much, that they may risk even larger losses so as to avoid a certain (moderate) loss. Preferring to lose $500 for sure to a 50%–50% bet on losing $1,000 (or nothing) is an example of such behavior.

Why do we tend to be so loss averse? There are many possible explanations. While in general we may not know what level of performance we can strive for, a level that we have already obtained in the past seems possible. Hence, it seems like a good idea not to let ourselves slip below it. Also, losing something we had may imply losing face in a social environment; others around us may think that we are on the decline and that they would better associate with competitors. Hence it makes sense that we do not like to lose, and that it is particularly painful to experience deterioration in our performance, or to feel that we made silly decisions.

Is this rational? Again, the answer is subjective. And, as in the case of the endowment effect, it may well depend on the type of application. Consider the following three scenarios.

Scenario 1: I am a politician. I pushed for a project that has so far cost $500,000. It was a bad idea. My advisors tell me that maybe it's time to drop it. There is a possibility of investing another $500,000 in it, and then it may pay off, roughly justifying the total investment; but it is equally likely to be an even bigger fiasco, burying $1,000,000 in total. What should I do?

Scenario 2: I am married, and I'm in charge of the family's finances. I made an investment of $5,000 in a friend's business. It looks in bad shape. My friend tells me that he needs more money invested, or it's all lost. I can invest an additional $5,000, which, with probability 50%, will save the business and give me my initial investment back, or, with probability 50%, be lost as well. Should I invest more and risk more or cut my losses?

Scenario 3: The same as Scenario 2, but this time I'm single.

Let's start with Scenario 1. As a politician, it may be a very bad idea to go back to my voters and say, "Remember these half a million dollars? Well, err, this was a bad idea. We lost them. But vote for me again and I'll make better decisions next term." It sounds like a better idea to say, "Sure, this is a big and important project, and we had some complications, but we need to stay our course and get this thing done." At the very least, the second idea buys me some time, whereas the first one looks like political suicide.

In fact, for the politician the payoff may not be the amount of money spent, but the probability of staying in office. Admitting a failure, or a loss, decreases this probability dramatically. Hence it may be perfectly rational for the politician to avoid such confessions, that is, to be loss averse.

Next consider Scenario 2. Here it's my money I'm dealing with, but I have a wife who may or may not think I'm smart. If I admit a loss, I'm going to lose face, and she may not trust my judgment in other decisions. I'm unlikely to be dismissed as a husband, but there is some similarity between my case and the politician's: we both have an audience of "constituency," waiting to see what we have done for them lately.

Finally, consider Scenario 3. Here I'm all by myself, and I have no one to fool. I can tell myself, "Yes, I can go on investing so as not to admit a failure, but I already know that this hasn't been such a smart decision, so who am I fooling? Maybe it's wiser to cut my losses."

I believe that most people would find loss aversion perfectly reasonable for the politician, but not so rational for themselves (in

Scenario 3). Scenario 2 is a mixed case, and some people may find loss aversion rational for them in such a scenario, while others probably won't. Again, you don't have to make a sweeping decision, whether loss aversion is a phenomenon you're going to reject or one you're willing to live with as rational: it is quite possible that in some cases loss aversion will be rational for you, while in others it won't.

Exercises

1. Assume that you are indifferent between getting $700 and getting $1,000 with probability 80% (and otherwise nothing). Assume also that you are indifferent between getting $300 and getting **$700** (not $1,000 this time!) with probability 60% (and otherwise nothing). Consider lottery A, which gives you $1,000 with probability 2/3 (and otherwise nothing), and lottery B, which gives you a 50%–50% bet between $300 and $700. If you follow von Neumann–Morgenstern's theory, you should:
   a. Prefer A to B.
   b. Prefer B to A.
   c. Be indifferent between A and B.
   d. One cannot tell based on the data.

   _____

   _____

   _____

2. Mary likes the von Neumann–Morgenstern's axioms and she would like to make decisions in accordance with these axioms. By careful introspection, she has decided that she would be indifferent between
      $400 for sure and a 50% probability of obtaining $1,000 (otherwise nothing); and also between

$600 for sure and an 80% probability of obtaining $1,000 (otherwise nothing).

Mary is offered a bet among ($0, $400, $600, $1,000) with equal chances (25% each) for a cost of $400. Should she prefer the bet or should she prefer to keep her $400?

_____

_____

_____

3. A state lottery sells tickets for a cost of $1 each. The ticket has a probability of 1/(2,400,000) of winning $1,000,000, and otherwise nothing.
   a. What is the expected profit of the state from each ticket sold?
   b. In the hope of increasing profits, the state considers increasing the award to $2,000,000 and reducing the probability of winning to 1/(4,800,000). A statistician said that it's not worth the trouble, because the expected profit remains precisely the same. What do you think?

_____

_____

_____

4. It is often argued that the value function in Kahneman and Tversky's prospect theory is convex in the domain of losses, that is, individuals behave in a risk loving way when it comes to losses. How can this be reconciled with the fact that people buy insurance (where premiums exceed expected losses)?

_____

_____

_____

Notes

1 Jacob cunningly received their father's blessing, which was Esau's birthright as he was the firstborn. When they met, Esau was heading a powerful army. However, this particular episode had a happy ending.

2 Bernoulli, D. (1738) Exposition of a new theory on the measurement of risk. *Econometrica*, 22 (1954), 23–36.

3 The terms "risk" and "uncertainty" for this distinction were suggested by Knight, F. H. (1921) *Risk, Uncertainty, and Profit*. Houghton Mifflin.

4 von Neumann, J. and Morgenstern, O. (1944) *Theory of Games and Economic Behavior*. Princeton University Press.

5 See, for example, Mehra, R. and Prescott, E. C. (1985) The equity premium: a puzzle. *Journal of Monetary Economics*, 15, 145–161.

6 This is known as Jensen's inequality.

7 Kahneman, D. and Tversky, A. (1979) Prospect theory: an analysis of decision under risk. *Econometrica*, 47, 263–291.

8 Allais, M. (1953) Le comportement de l'homme rationnel devant le risque: critique des postulats et axiomes de l'Ecole Americaine. *Econometrica*, 21, 503–546.

9 Kahneman and Tversky (1979), see note 7.

10 This version is not the one published in Kahneman and Tversky's original paper, nor the one to which they later adapted the theory. This formula had been suggested also by Edwards (see note 11). Details are beyond the scope of this book.

11 Edwards, W. (1954) The theory of decision making. *Psychological Bulletin*, 51, 380–417.

12 Helson, H. (1947) Adaptation-level as frame of reference for prediction of psychophysical data. *American Journal of Psychology*, 60, 1–29.

13 Simon, H. A. (1955) A behavioral model of rational choice. *Quarterly Journal of Economics*, 69, 99–118.

5

Decisions under Uncertainty

Introduction

The previous chapter dealt with probabilities that are explicitly given to us, or that can be assumed known. It is time to move on to problems in which probabilities are not given, or cannot be inferred from existing statistical data. Observe that these problems include many of the more important ones in our lives. The probability of a stock market crash over the next month is not written anywhere, and cannot be easily inferred from existing data. Similarly, the eruption of war in the Middle East over the next two years is another example of an event that is uncertain in the sense that we do not know its probability. The same holds also for many personal decisions, such as the choice of a career or a spouse. When you get married no one provides you with the probability that you will end up divorcing, and relying on general statistics to infer this probability is not very promising. And similar uncertainty exists when you consider the possibility of success of a new business venture, or a new career path, and so forth.

One idea that we describe but also critically examine here is that the mathematical machinery of probability theory can be used to

Making Better Decisions, by Itzhak Gilboa © 2011 John Wiley & Sons, Inc.

reason about uncertainty, even when probabilities are not given. The idea is that we can use a probability function that need not be "real" in any sense, but that reflects our beliefs, and use it to make better decisions. We have already encountered this idea in Chapter 2, when we noted that the use of *subjective probability* can make us immune to the conjunction fallacy (rating Linda being a bank teller as less likely than being a bank teller who is also active in a feminist movement).

It is an interesting historical fact that Blaise Pascal, often considered to be the most important figure in the invention of probability theory, was also the first person who used subjective probability. In his famous wager, Pascal takes a very modern approach to the problem of faith. Rather than trying to prove that God exists, as did many before and after him, Pascal skipped the metaphysical problem of God's existence and discussed instead the decision problem of the individual human being: to choose to believe in God or not. Pascal's main argument for believing in God relies on the assumption that the payoff in the afterlife is infinite, while anything you may enjoy on Earth is finite. Therefore, he argues, no matter how small is the probability that God exists, you are better off believing in Him. Clearly, the "probability that God exists" refers to subjective probability, namely, a way to quantify uncertainty. Moreover, Pascal's argument is one of maximizing expectation.[1] Hence, Pascal was the first person to suggest the notion of expected utility maximization, and he used it in the context of subjective probabilities.

The following problems deal with issues that are slightly more mundane. But they will lead to the same questions: how and when can we use the machinery of probability theory to quantify our beliefs and make better decisions in the face of uncertainty?

Problems

In the following ten problems you are asked to choose between "bets." A bet yields a particular outcome if a specified event occurs.

Some of the events are real-life ones, and some are defined by chance mechanisms, such as coins and roulette wheels.

In Problems 5.1–5.10 you are promised the same outcome conditional on events that may be known only in the future. In each such problem, imagine that the payoff is obtained at the same time, whether you choose A or B.

Problem 5.1

Do you prefer to get $100 if
A: It will snow on February 1st;
B: A roulette wheel yields the outcome 3?

Problem 5.2

Do you prefer to get $100 if
A: The student next to you gets A in this class;
B: Two consecutive tosses of a fair coin come up Head?

Problem 5.3

Do you prefer to get $100 if
A: Your next flight is delayed by more than an hour;
B: A roulette wheel yields an outcome in the range 0–5?

Problem 5.4

Do you prefer to get $100 if
A: The Dow Jones Industrial Average (DJIA) is at least at its current value at the end of the year;
B: A toss of a fair coin is Head?

Problem 5.5

Do you prefer to get $100 if
A: The next president of the United States is a Democrat;
B: A toss of a fair coin is Head?

Problem 5.6

Do you prefer to get $100 if
A: It will *not* snow on February 1st;
B: A roulette wheel yields an outcome different than 24?

Problem 5.7

Do you prefer to get $100 if
A: The student next to you gets less than A in this class;
B: A roulette wheel yields an outcome less than 24?

Problem 5.8

Do you prefer to get $100 if
A: Your next flight is on time;
B: In two consecutive tosses of a fair coin there is at least one Head?

Problem 5.9

Do you prefer to get $100 if
A: The DJIA is below its current value at the end of the year;
B: A toss of a fair coin is Head?

Problem 5.10

Do you prefer to get $100 if
A: The next president of the United States is a Republican;
B: A toss of a fair coin is Head?

Problem 5.11

You are offered two assets, based on the percentage of change in the DJIA between today and tomorrow. Let this percentage change be denoted by Δ. Do you prefer to get:

A: $1,000   if $1\% < \Delta$
     $2,000   if $0 < \Delta \leq 1\%$
     -$1,000   if $-0.5\% < \Delta \leq 0$
     $0   if $\Delta \leq -0.5\%$

or

B: −$1,000   if $0.8\% < \Delta$
    $1,000   if $-0.1\% < \Delta \leq 0.8\%$
    $500   if $-0.7\% < \Delta \leq -0.1\%$
    $2,000   if $\Delta \leq -0.7\%$

Problem 5.12

Consider the following version of the TV game "Let's Make a Deal": there are three doors, marked A, B, and C, and behind one of them there is a prize (a car). Behind the two other doors there is no prize (a goat). Based on past plays of the game, you can safely assume that the car is behind doors A, B, and C with equal probabilities.

You are asked to name a door. Before you open it, the moderator (Monty Hall), who knows where the car is, opens a door. He has to open a door that (i) differs from the one you named; and (ii) does not have the car behind it. (Since there are three doors, he can always do that.) Now you are given a choice: you can either open the first door you named ("stick") or open the other door still closed ("switch"). You get the prize behind the door you decide to open, and your goal is to maximize the probability of getting the car. What should you do?

a. Stick.
b. Switch.
c. It doesn't matter.

Problem 5.13

Comment on the following dialog.

> MARTINE: The question now is, should we cut prices.
> VERONIQUE: If you do, you probably get a higher market share, but lower profit per customer. It's a familiar trade-off.

MARTINE: Yes, but it depends on the competition. And I don't know whether they will or won't cut prices.

VERONIQUE: I'm not so sure you should care. If the competition cuts prices, you have to cut prices as well. If they don't, you're better off cutting prices and being the cheapest.

MARTINE: How come? By this reasoning, we should sell at zero prices.

VERONIQUE: Well, maybe not zero prices, but close to zero profit. It happens. It's related to the "Prisoner's Dilemma": you may both be better off if you don't cut prices, but it is rational for each one to cut their prices.

MARTINE: Hmmm.

VERONIQUE: Yes, the point is that whatever the others do, you should cut prices. Hence you don't care what they do, and you might as well cut prices now.

Problem 5.14

There are two urns in front of you, each containing 100 balls. Urn A contains 50 red balls and 50 black balls. Urn B contains 100 balls, and you are told that each ball is either red or black, but you do not know how many of the 100 balls are red and how many are black.

You are asked to choose an urn (A or B), and a color (red or black). Once you announce your choice, a ball will be drawn at random from the urn you named. If it is the color you named, you get $100. Otherwise you get nothing.

There are, therefore, four possible choices:

AR – betting on a red ball drawn out of urn A
AB – betting on a black ball drawn out of urn A
BR – betting on a red ball drawn out of urn B
BB – betting on a black ball drawn out of urn B

Decisions under Uncertainty

What are your preferences between the following pairs of bets?
a. AR ___ AB
b. BR ___ BB
c. AR ___ BR
d. AB ___ BB

Problem 5.15

There is an urn containing 90 balls. Each ball can be red, blue, or yellow. You are also told that there are precisely 30 red balls in the urn. Hence, the remaining 60 balls are blue or yellow, but you don't know how many are blue and how many are yellow.

A ball is to be drawn at random from the urn. You are offered choices between pairs of bets, where "betting on an event" implies winning $1,000 if the event occurs, and nothing otherwise:

a. Betting on the ball being red
   vs.
   betting on the ball being blue
b. Betting on the ball being red
   vs.
   betting on the ball being yellow
c. Betting on the ball being *not* red
   vs.
   betting on the ball being *not* blue
d. Betting on the ball being *not* red
   vs.
   betting on the ball being *not* yellow.

Problem 5.16

Suppose that I am about to undergo a medical operation. I ask my doctor what the probability of success is. How can my doctor provide me with an objective answer?

_____

_____

Problem 5.17

Suppose that I'm interested in an investment whose value depends on the possibility of war. I consult an expert on international relations, and ask him what the probability of war in the Middle East in the next year is. How can the expert provide an objective answer?

_____

_____

Subjective Probability

In the previous chapter we dealt with decisions under risk, that is, where probabilities were given to us in the description of the problem. "Given" probabilities are encountered in games of chance, such as casino games, state lotteries, and psychological experiments. There are many other circumstances where the probabilities are not generated by a chance device, such as a roulette wheel, but they can still be assumed to be more or less known, or "objective." For example, when we deal with an insurance problem, we can look at statistical data and see what the empirical frequencies of various events are. These empirical frequencies are often taken to be the probabilities of these events occurring again in the future. If the events in the past, as well as those that are awaiting us in the future, can be assumed i.i.d. (identically and independently distributed), and if there are many of them, this appears to be a reasonable definition, and the empirical frequency can be used to define objective probability.

However, many important decisions in our lives depend on events that are not repeated in the same way, so that the assumption of i.i.d. events doesn't hold. When we consider the stock market behavior over the next week, we can't assume that it will have the same distribution as in previous weeks. Things change in the world, and no two weeks are identical. Further, the very fact that last week the stock market ended up in a certain way is a piece of information that changes our predictions for the coming week. Thus, consecutive events are not even causally independent, let alone statistically independent. When we consider, for example, the possibility of war in the Middle East, we can't simply resort to past statistics for a definition of probabilities, both because no two instances are identical, and because the very fact that a certain war occurred changes the probability that future wars will.

These complications are not restricted to "big" events such as war and peace, crashes and booms. An individual's choice of a career path, or their decision to get married, is also a "big" event in the sense that it is never repeated in the very same way, and often not even with causal independence between consecutive occurrences. Thus, if Mary is asked to assess the probability that she will succeed in finding a job as a lawyer, if she decides to start her studies now, and if John wonders what is the probability that he will want to move and sell his house in the next two years, they cannot simply look at past data and use empirical frequencies as probabilities.

As mentioned in the introduction, Pascal had already used the machinery of probability theory to sort out intuition and reason about uncertainty where no objective probabilities exist. The idea is that even if the probabilities that you assign to events will not be objective or scientifically estimated, the very discipline imposed by quantifying uncertainty may be useful. The probabilities that you end up with are bound to be subjective, because you don't have nearly enough information to come up with scientific or objective assessments. But the machinery of probability theory, used for *subjective probability*, guarantees that your beliefs will be internally coherent. You may not be right when we compare your assessments with actual data, but at least you will not be so silly as to contradict yourself.

Suppose that you like this idea and try to assess your own subjective probabilities for various events, that is, try to put your beliefs, intuitions, and hunches into numbers. How would you do that? One possibility is to compare the probability of events for which probability is not given with the probability of events for which it is. And to make things concrete, it is often suggested that you relate the questions of likelihood to decision problems. That is, rather than asking "which event seems more plausible?" we will often ask, "which event would you prefer to bet on?" Let's see how this works in Problems 5.1–5.10.

Let's begin with Problem 5.1:

Problem 5.1

Do you prefer to get $100 if

A: It will snow on February 1st;
B: A roulette wheel yields the outcome 3?

The probability of (B) is objectively known. It is 1/37 (or 1/38, depending on the type of roulette wheel we have). The probability of (A) is not known. But if you prefer to get $100 if it snows than if the roulette wheel yields the outcome 3, you probably think that the probability of snow on February 1st is higher than 1/37. To be precise, this is going to be the definition of your subjective probability: even if you will state some other beliefs, what we really care about are the decisions you make. Therefore, if we find that you make decisions *as if* your subjective probability of snow were higher than 1/37, that's good enough for our purposes.

Clearly, if you prefer to bet on (B) than on (A), we will conclude that your subjective probability of snow is (or should be defined as) lower than 1/37. And if you're indifferent, we've found the precise value of your subjective probability of snow on February 1st. The general method is to replace the objectively quantifiable event (here, (B)) with another objectively quantifiable one until we reach this indifference, and thus "calibrate," or measure, your subjective probability.

This process surely reminds you of the calibration of utility under risk. There, too, we use objectively given probabilities as a way to scale, or measure, a subjective magnitude. The difference is that in the previous chapter we were trying to quantify utility, and here we are quantifying subjective probability. But the process is similar. And another similarity is that, for this procedure to be successful, your preferences should have a certain degree of internal coherence, so that your answers to simple questions would not be contradictory, and will be valid also for your decisions in more complex situations.

Let us see what type of internal coherence is relevant in the case of subjective probabilities. Compare your answer in 5.1 with your answer in Problem 5.6:

Problem 5.6

Do you prefer to get $100 if

A: It will *not* snow on February 1st;
B: A roulette wheel yields an outcome different than 24?

Here the question is whether the outcome of no-snow on February 1st is more or less likely than the outcome of the roulette wheel being different than 24. But the latter is known – it is 36/37. Thus, we see that there are certain constraints on the answers you can provide, should your beliefs be represented by subjective probabilities. For example, if you choose (A) in both Problems 5.1 and 5.6, we will not be able to use probabilities to capture your beliefs. Indeed, choosing (A) in 5.1 means that, in your eyes,

$$\text{Prob (snow)} > \text{Prob (outcome 3)} = 1/37$$

and this means that

$$\text{Prob (no-snow)} = 1 - \text{Prob (snow)} < 36/37$$

whereas choosing (A) in 5.6 means that

$$\text{Prob}\left(\text{no-snow}\right) > \text{Prob}\left(\text{outcome different from } 24\right) = 36 \, / \, 37$$

(Notice that I assumed here that your preferences were strict. If you were indifferent in both cases and, shrugging your shoulders, gave me a random answer, no contradiction arises.)

You may now ask yourself whether indeed you chose (A) in both. Or (B) in both – this will generate precisely the same problem, only with the inequality signs reversed. If you didn't, namely if your choices were (A) in 5.1 and (B) in 5.6, or vice versa, you can go on to try to assess your subjective probability of snow on February 1st. If, however, your choices were inconsistent with the notion of subjective probability, you will have to make a meta-decision, of whether you would like to make decisions that are compatible with subjective probabilities or not. As in any other problem we discuss, it is up to you to decide whether a particular mode of behavior is rational for you. If the answer is negative, we can find a formal model that will help you avoid this type of behavior. But you should first be convinced that this model is truly what you like to use for your own decision making, rather than a model that some theorists happen to be excited about.

I suggest that you withhold judgment on this question for a while. Much of my own research career has been devoted to it, and this is the part of classical decision theory that I find the least compelling from a normative point of view. Let us first look at a few more examples and then discuss this issue again.

Compare your answers to the following two problems:

Problem 5.2

Do you prefer to get $100 if

A: The student next to you gets A in this class;
B: Two consecutive tosses of a fair coin come up Head?

Decisions under Uncertainty

Problem 5.7

Do you prefer to get $100 if

A: The student next to you gets less than A in this class;
B: A roulette wheel yields an outcome less than 24?

Problem 5.2 basically asks you to compare

Prob (student gets A) and Prob (two consecutive Heads) = 25%

While 5.7 asks you to compare

Prob (student doesn't get A) and Prob (outcome < 24) = 24 / 37

which is equivalent to comparing

Prob (student gets A) and Prob (outcome ≥ 24) = 13 / 37s ≅ 35%

A pattern of answers that is inconsistent with subjective probabilities would be to choose (B) in 5.2 and (B) in 5.7. To see this, observe that choosing (B) in 5.2 means that

Prob (student gets A) < Prob (two consecutive Heads) = 25%

while choosing (B) in 5.7 implies

Prob (student doesn't get A) < Prob (outcome < 24)
 = 24 / 37 ≅ 65%

or

Prob (student gets A) > 1 − 65% = 35%

However, the three other combinations of answers are consistent with subjective probabilities: if you choose (B) in 5.2 and (A) in 5.7, this is compatible with

Prob (student gets A) < 25%

and if you choose (A) in 5.2 and (B) in 5.7, you probably believe that

146

Prob (student gets A) > 35%

Importantly – as opposed to the example of Problems 5.1 and 5.6 – you can here choose (A) in 5.2 as well as (A) in 5.6, and this would imply that your subjective probability satisfies

25% < Prob (student gets A) < 35%

Continuing in this way, if there is a subjective probability that guides our decisions, we will be able to find it.

Next consider the following pair:

Problem 5.3

Do you prefer to get $100 if

A: Your next flight is delayed by more than an hour;
B: A roulette wheel yields an outcome in the range 0–5?

Problem 5.8

Do you prefer to get $100 if

A: Your next flight is on time;
B: In two consecutive tosses of a fair coin there is at least one Head?

Here, again, we have well-defined, objective probabilities in option (B) of each problem, and an event with no objective probability in option (A). This pair differs from the previous ones in two ways. First, the events in options (A) of the two problems are disjoint, but they are not complementary: if your flight is delayed by more than an hour, it is evidently not on time, but it can be neither.

The second new feature in this example is that you might prefer (A) in 5.3 not because you think that it is very likely that your flight is delayed by more than an hour, but because you think that you might need the extra cash in this case – for instance, if, due to this delay, you miss your connection to a different airline, and have to pay extra for the change of ticket. If this is the reason you choose (A) in 5.3, this choice doesn't tell us much about your beliefs.

This is not a trivial issue. In fact, it could also apply in the previous examples. If you go back to Problem 5.1, suppose that you see someone preferring (A) to (B) – is it because they really believe that the snow on February 1st is more likely than the roulette wheel yielding 3, or is it perhaps because, should it snow, they will need to buy a new coat, and this is why they prefer the money in this case? And maybe it's because they have a distaste for casinos and therefore prefer (A)? Our goal in introducing these preference questions was to make the notion of "likelihood" or "plausibility" concrete. But if, by doing so, we introduce a new bias, having to do with the interaction of the outcome with the event, we get rather skewed results.[2]

So let us take this opportunity to clarify the nature of the exercise: when you're asked to choose among choices as in these problems, you are implicitly asked to imagine that the outcomes promised do not change, and do not become more or less desirable as a result of the event with which they are associated. Often, this will be easy to imagine. But there are also situations – involving medical decisions, life and death issues, and the like – where this becomes harder to imagine. For instance, if I try to assess the probability of my death for the sake of a life insurance decision, it is hard to imagine how much fun it would be to get $100 when I'm six feet under. With all due respect to my children's well-being, I suppose that I will not enjoy the money the same way when I'm dead as when I'm alive.

Therefore, when it comes to decisions involving various life and health risks, we will need more refined procedures to try to elicit our subjective probabilities. In most other problems we will try to imagine getting various outcomes, or payoffs, ignoring our special needs given the event in question, as well as ignoring any ethical and moral issues having to do with enjoying the payoff when this particular event occurs.

Going back to the problems, we find that in 5.3 I should prefer (A) if (and only if)

$$\text{Prob}\left(\text{a delay of at least 1 hour}\right) > 6 / 37 \cong 16\%$$

whereas in 5.8 I should prefer (A) if (and only if)

Prob (zero delay) > 75%

Because the two events on the right hand sides are disjoint but not complementary, the only constraint we have is that the probability you assign to (A) in 5.3 and the probability you assign to (A) in 5.8 together do not exceed 1. Since the two right hand sides together are less than 1, there is no contradiction in choosing (A) in both. You may, for instance, believe that the probability of no delay at all is 80%, but that, if there is a delay, it will be of an hour or more, so that the probability of such a delay is 20%.

You may also choose (B) in both problems, for instance, if you believe that the flight is very likely to be delayed, but by less than an hour. In fact, you may even assign to this event probability 1, implying

Prob (a delay of at least 1 hour), Prob (zero delay) = 0

Of course, it's not clear how you can be so sure that the flight will be delayed, but by no more than an hour, but this is still consistent with the discipline put upon us by subjective probabilities. Importantly, the exercise we are performing here is checking whether your beliefs can be represented in a probabilistic way, not asking how you might justify these beliefs.

Next, consider the following pair:

Problem 5.4

Do you prefer to get $100 if

A: The DJIA is at least at its current value at the end of the year;
B: A toss of a fair coin is Head?

Problem 5.9

Do you prefer to get $100 if

A: The DJIA is below its current value at the end of the year;
B: A toss of a fair coin is Head?

This is a relatively simple example. The events (A) in the two problems are complements of each other. If you are to assign to them subjective probabilities, they should add up to 1. The events in (B) are identical, with an objective probability of 50%. This is almost precisely the case in Problems 5.5 and 5.10:

Problem 5.5

Do you prefer to get $100 if

A: The next president of the United States is a Democrat;
B: A toss of a fair coin is Head?

Problem 5.10

Do you prefer to get $100 if

A: The next president of the United States is a Republican;
B: A toss of a fair coin is Head?

– with the minor difference that in this pair the two events are not complements, strictly speaking, since the United States may elect a president who doesn't belong to either major party.

It is often the case that people prefer (B) in both 5.4 and 5.9, or in both 5.5 and 5.10. Such choices are incompatible with representation of beliefs by subjective probabilities. The same would apply to choosing (A) in both 5.4 and 5.9 (or in both 5.5 and 5.10). However, this is a much less common pattern of choice. We will discuss these phenomena when we deal with difficulties with probabilities later on.

In the meantime, you may turn to Problem 5.11. Try to apply this technique to measure your own subjective probability for the events in question. Then apply the technique of Chapter 4 to estimate your utility function. Finally, use your subjective probabilities and your utility function to find which decision yields a higher expected utility in this problem. As you can see, the principles that we have considered can help you think about this relatively complex problem, based on your decisions in simpler ones. Do you find the resulting decisions palatable?

Learning From the Fact We Know

Our next two sections have to deal with the question of what are we assigning probabilities to? Typically, we think of a probability model, in which there are possible scenarios, sometimes called *states of nature* or *states of the world*, of which precisely one will materialize. Events are collections of such states. If we assign a probability to each state, we can compute the probability of an event by summing up the probabilities of the states belonging to it. In particular, if we consider the "sure event," consisting of all states, we should have the probability summing up to 1. All this seems natural and familiar. However, sometimes some care is needed in defining the "states." Let us begin with Problem 5.12:

> Consider the following version of the TV game "Let's Make a Deal": there are three doors, marked A, B, and C, and behind one of them there is a prize (a car). Behind the two other doors there is no prize (a goat). Based on past plays of the game, you can safely assume that the car is behind doors A, B, and C with equal probabilities.
>
> You are asked to name a door. Before you open it, the moderator (Monty Hall), who knows where the car is, opens a door. He has to open a door that (i) differs from the one you named; and (ii) does not have the car behind it. (Since there are three doors, he can always do that.) Now you are given a choice: you can either open the first door you named ("stick") or open the other door still closed ("switch"). You get the prize behind the door you decide to open, and your goal is to maximize the probability of getting the car. What should you do?

Let us first convince ourselves that the strategy "switch" is better than "stick." In fact, "switch" guarantees us a probability of 2/3 of winning the car, while "stick" gives us a probability of only 1/3. This might be more intuitive if we observe that "switch" means "always switch," and it results in different doors depending on Monty Hall's choice.

Let us be more concrete. Suppose that you are the contestant and that your initial choice was door A. Clearly, the same analysis applies to any initial choice: because the three doors are, a priori, equally likely to have the car behind them, the situation is symmetric with respect to this initial choice.

Strategy "stick" means opening door A, regardless of Monty's choice. Thus, it has probability of 1/3 of yielding the car, namely, the probability that the initial choice happened to be lucky. By contrast, strategy "switch" means different doors: if Monty opens B, "switch" will mean "open C"; if he opens C, "switch" will mean "open B." And the point is that "switch" wins *whenever* the original choice was wrong. That is, if the car is behind B or C, "switch" will get it. Let us verify that this is correct:

Assume the car is behind B. Monty sees:

A	B	C
goat	car	goat

Since you named A, Monty has to open C. So you get to see:

A	B	C
closed	closed	open

and "switching" (to the other closed door) leads you to the car.
And if the car is behind C, Monty sees:

A	B	C
goat	goat	car

Since you named A, Monty has to open B. So you get to see:

A	B	C
closed	open	closed

and "switching" (to the other closed door) leads you to the car again.

Table 5.1 Car acts and states; "1" stands for the car, "0" for a goat.

		States (car is behind…)		
	Probability	1/3	1/3	1/3
	Payoff	A	B	C
Acts	Stick	1	0	0
	Switch	0	1	1

Obviously, "switch" will not get the car if it is actually behind A, and this is precisely when "stick" wins. We get the evaluation matrix shown in Table 5.1.

This is an opportunity to stop for a minute and look at this matrix. It is, in fact, the first decision matrix we see in this book. In such a matrix we separate the choices that are up to us from those that aren't. We typically use the rows to designate our choices: *acts, strategies,* or *courses of action,* that specify our decisions. Importantly, each such act should tell us what to do in each and every possible eventuality. Thus, the act (or "strategy") "switch" tells us what to do when we get additional information. Our choice of a strategy can be made a priori, before we get the information, and it specifies what to do given any possible information we may get later on.

The columns in such a matrix are the states of nature, or states of the world, and they can be thought of as the strategies of nature in the game: anything that does not depend on us. Generally, a *state* should specify all that is uncertain: which random events occur and which do not, what choices other agents make, and so forth. It is important that we conceptualize the choice of a row (by the decision maker) and the choice of a column (by nature, as well as by other agents) as causally independent.

Finally, the entries inside the matrix reflect the outcomes: what will happen if we choose the respective row, and nature chooses the respective column. Often, we summarize an outcome by its utility, which in this case is assumed to be the probability of winning the car. When we have probabilities over the states of the world, we can use them to compute the expected utility corresponding to each act. In our problem, we are given the probabilities of the three states: 1/3 for each. Hence it is easy to verify that the expected payoff of "stick" is 1/3, while that of "switch" is 2/3.

Even if you agree with this analysis, you may still be troubled. You named door A. Suppose that Monty Hall opens door B. You are faced with the choice between (switching to) C and (sticking to) A. Why would door C be more likely to conceal the car than door A? How come the probability of door B suddenly "shifted" to door C? This is troubling indeed. We will try to understand this issue in two steps. First, let us try to see why, intuitively, door C is more likely to conceal the car than door A. Second, we'll have to understand what's wrong with simple Bayesian updating, and this will be the main lesson from this example.

To see why door C is more likely to be the right one, we have to recall that the "other" door, which was left shut and to which you consider switching, did not have to be door C. This "other" door could have been B or C. The a priori probability that the specific door C conceals the car is equal to the probability that A does. But now we know that C survived a certain selection process. A priori, we should think about the "other" door, which is actually a random variable. In this particular realization, the random variable happens to be C; but it could have been B as well.

It is useful to point out that the rules of the game are such that Monty Hall helps you by removing one of the bad choices you can make. He is not allowed to open the door that truly does conceal the car. This means that after he opens a door you have only two possible choices, rather than three. That is, you have fewer possible mistakes to make. This means that you're better off with him opening one door than you were at the outset. But this is not quite enough: since one bad choice is crossed out, you would have believed that both the remaining ones are now more likely to be successful. Why do we argue that only the "other" door is more likely to conceal the car?

The reason is that Monty Hall is not allowed to open your original choice, A. When you compare the doors left shut, A and C, you know why A is shut: Monty Hall couldn't have opened it according to the rules of the game. By contrast, for door C to remain shut, it had to pass a more demanding test. It is as if it were harder for the other door to remain closed than for yours. Put differently, the fact that these two doors, A and C, remained closed does not provide any additional information about door A, but it does provide some additional information about door C.

To be absolutely convinced, suppose there were 1,000 doors, and Monty had to open 998 of them, but couldn't open yours. You name door 378. Monty goes around, and opens 998 doors. When he's done, you see 998 goats and two closed doors: 378 and 752. Where do you think the car is: behind 378, which you anyway knew was going to remain closed, or behind 752, which was singled out by Monty, out of all the other 999 doors?

These arguments hopefully make the conclusion slightly more intuitive. But we are still left with the question of what's wrong with the reasoning that says that the two strategies are equivalent? We won't be able to have a good night's sleep until we understand what is wrong with the other reasoning, which goes as follows:

We had a prior probability of 1/3 on each door:

A	B	C
1/3	1/3	1/3

Now assume that Monty opens door B, and we see a goat. We have learnt "not B," or, if you wish, the event {A, C}. Standard Bayesian updating of the prior probability given this event would yield

$$P(A \mid \{A, C\}) = P(A \cap \{A, C\}) / P(\{A, C\})$$
$$= P(A) / P(\{A, C\}) = (1/3)/(2/3) = 1/2$$

... and similarly for C. In other words, the standard way of updating prior to posterior beliefs tells us that we have a 50%–50% probability of finding the car behind door A and behind door C. Therefore, there is no reason to switch. What's wrong with this? And how do we reconcile this conclusion with the analysis above, which showed that switching is better?

The answer is that this calculation is a perfectly correct analysis of an incorrect model. The problem is not in the mathematics; the problem is in the modeling. The model we used here employs three states of the world: the car is behind A, B, or C. This formulation makes the implicit assumption that all that matters is where the car is. This turns out to be a wrong assumption in this story. Sometimes, *how* we learn information, or *the very fact that we have indeed received a piece of information*, might be informative in its own right. Here, the fact that Monty Hall provided a piece of information, namely, that the car is not behind door B, tells us that the car is indeed not behind door B, but it also tells us more.

Generally, we should learn from this example that we should be sensitive not only to the information we have, but to the very fact we have it. We should ask ourselves what other information, if any, we could have received, and what does it mean that we know what we know rather than something else we could have known.[3] To capture all this in a Bayesian analysis, we have to first make sure that the state space we work with is rich enough to describe the information we have received, how we acquired it, who might have made certain choices to provide us with this information, and so on.

A correct analysis of the Monty Hall game would take into account both where the car is and which door Monty opens. Still assuming you initially chose door A, we would need nine, rather than three, relevant states (Table 5.2). Table 5.2 is not a decision matrix. Each entry here is a state of the world, that is, a column in a decision matrix. But since the car may be behind any of three doors, and Monty Hall might (conceivably) open any one of three doors, we have nine states, and the matrix in Table 5.2 will help us assess their probabilities. Let's start.

When we add up the (as yet unwritten) probability numbers in a given row, we will get at the right margin the overall probability of the car being behind door A/B/C. These probabilities are known to be 1/3 each. Observe that a single state of the world in the previous

Table 5.2 Car is behind and Monty opens, phase 1.

		Monty opens			
		A	B	C	Total
Car	A				1/3
is	B				1/3
behind	C				1/3
	Total				1

Table 5.3 Car is behind and Monty opens, phase 2.

		Monty opens			
		A	B	C	Total
Car	A	0			1/3
is	B	0	0		1/3
behind	C	0		0	1/3
	Total	0			1

(wrong) analysis corresponds here to an entire row. Indeed, the overall probability of 1/3 for each row in this formulation mirrors the probability of 1/3 for each state of the world in the three-state model we discarded.

We know that Monty can't open door A (that you named). This means that the probabilities of all states in the first column are 0. Similarly, Monty is not allowed to open the door hiding the car. This means that the states of the world along the diagonal (where he opens door A and the car is behind A, or he opens B and the car is behind B, etc.) also have zero probability. Putting these two together we obtain the matrix in Table 5.3.

Observe that the total (or "marginal") probability of the first column is zero, as it is the sum of zeros. Indeed, this reflects our belief that Monty Hall will not open door A. Next, notice that what we have filled in so far implies a unique way to complete the last two rows: if the car is behind B, which happens with probability 1/3, we

Table 5.4 Car is behind and Monty opens, phase 3.

		Monty opens			
		A	B	C	Total
Car	A	0			1/3
is	B	0	0	1/3	1/3
behind	C	0	1/3	0	1/3
	Total	0			1

can't put any probability mass in the first two columns (in this row), so we have to put the entire 1/3 in the third column. By a similar consideration, the entire probability of the third row ("the car is behind C") has to be in the second column (Table 5.4).

The fact that we had no freedom in splitting these probabilities (of 1/3 each) in their respective rows reflects the fact that the rules of the game do not leave Monty Hall any choice in opening doors in the case your initial choice was wrong. By contrast, if your initial choice, A, happens to be right, Monty does have a choice between opening B or C. We're not quite sure what his rule would be in this case. Let us first make a simplifying assumption that, if the car is indeed behind A, he makes a random choice between B and C. This means that the probability of 1/3 of the top row is split equally between the last two columns, giving each of the two possible entries a probability of 1/6. With these in place, we can also compute the total ("marginal") probability of each column (Table 5.5).

Let us now see that the way we get information may be informative in and of itself. Assume that all you know is only that the car is not behind B. According to the rules of the game, you can't get this information: the only way to learn that the car is not behind B is to hear it from Monty Hall. But in order to clarify the point, assume that, hypothetically, you get this information and no more. For instance, assume that, the night before you participate in the show, your great-great-grandfather appears in your dream and

Table 5.5 Car is behind and Monty opens, phase 4.

		Monty opens			
		A	B	C	Total
Car	A	0	1/6	1/6	1/3
is	B	0	0	1/3	1/3
behind	C	0	1/3	0	1/3
	Total	0	1/2	1/2	1

Table 5.6 Car is behind and Monty opens, phase 5.

		Monty opens			
		A	B	C	Total
Car	A	0	1/6	1/6	1/3
is	B	0	0	1/3	1/3
behind	C	0	1/3	0	1/3
	Total	0	1/2	1/2	1

whispers, "My child, it's not B." You're not superstitious, but great-great-grandfathers do command respect, so you believe him. Importantly, the very fact that the information has been obtained is supposedly independent of the game (as opposed to the information provided by Monty Hall). In this case you'll be justified in having a simple Bayesian updating of the probability, conditional on the first and last rows, and you will have a 50%–50% posterior on A and C (Table 5.6).

However, this is not the case at hand: you didn't learn "not B" from some unrelated source, and "not B" does not summarize all you know. You also know that *Monty Hall opened door B*. So you should condition on the middle column, crossing out the other two (Table 5.7).

The middle column does, indeed, give zero probability to the second row (the car being behind door B). This means that, when

Table 5.7 Car is behind and Monty opens, phase 6.

		Monty opens			
		A	B	C	Total
Car	A	0	1/6	1/6	1/3
is	B	0	0	1/3	1/3
behind	C	0	1/3	0	1/3
	Total	0	1/2	1/2	1

Monty Hall opens door B, you indeed know that the car is not behind B. But it also changes the conditional probabilities of the other two rows. Indeed, the conditional probability of the first row is

$$P(\text{car behind A} \mid \text{MH opened B}) = (1/6)/(1/2) = 1/3$$

while the last row gets

$$P(\text{car behind C} \mid \text{MH opened B}) = (1/3)/(1/2) = 2/3$$

And according to this analysis you should indeed switch, because C has a probability 2/3 of having the car. Clearly the same would apply to door B if Monty Hall opened C.

This analysis was predicated on the assumption that, if you happened to be right in the initial guess, then, given the choice between B and C, Monty Hall randomizes. But what if he doesn't randomize with equal probabilities? Maybe he has some other rule? Suppose that your beliefs about his choice, based on a known or unknown rule, wholly or partly random, are summarized by a parameter α, between 0 and 1/3, which tells you how much of the probability mass of 1/3 resides in the middle column, and how much in the last one (Table 5.8).

Table 5.8 Car is behind and Monty opens, phase 7.

		Monty opens			
		A	B	C	Total
Car	A	0	α	$1/3 - \alpha$	1/3
is	B	0	0	1/3	1/3
behind	C	0	1/3	0	1/3
	Total	0	$1/3 + \alpha$	$2/3 - \alpha$	1

Table 5.9 Car is behind and Monty opens, phase 8.

		Monty opens			
		A	B	C	Total
Car	A	0	1/3	0	1/3
is	B	0	0	1/3	1/3
behind	C	0	1/3	0	1/3
	Total	0	2/3	1/3	1

Now the conditional probabilities of finding the car behind door B (if C is opened) or behind C (if B is opened) depend on your assumptions about Monty Hall in case he has a choice. For instance, if he always opens B when he can, we get the matrix in Table 5.9.

In this case, if Monty Hall opens door B, there is indeed no reason to switch: the conditional probabilities of A and C are 50%–50%. But if C is opened, the conditional probability puts the entire mass on door B. In this case not only do you have an incentive to switch, you are also certain that you're going to win the car by this switch. Note that our original calculation, stating that "switch" wins with probability 2/3, is valid in this case as well:

$$P(\text{wins}) = P(\text{opened B}) * P(\text{wins} \mid \text{opened B}) + P(\text{opened C})$$
$$* P(\text{wins} \mid \text{opened C}) = (2/3)*$$
$$(1/2) + (1/3) * 1 = 2/3$$

Table 5.10   Car is behind and Monty opens, phase 9.

| | | Monty opens | | | |
		A	B	C	Total
Car	A	0	1/6	1/6	1/3
is	B	1/6	0	1/6	1/3
behind	C	1/6	1/6	0	1/3
	Total	1/3	1/3	1/3	1

In fact, this is true for any α.

With this analysis, we can also see why it is so important that Monty Hall can't open the door you chose. If he could, assuming that he makes a random choice between the two doors that do not conceal the car, we would have had a matrix like that in Table 5.10, and in this matrix, indeed, there is no reason to switch: whatever column you condition on, the conditional probabilities over the two relevant rows are 50%–50%.

This was a little long. Let us focus on the main lessons of this example:

- It is extremely important to have the right model for your problem. If you start with an inappropriate model, you may have a perfect mathematical solution of the wrong problem.
- Typically, if you do have an inappropriate model, the mathematical analysis will give you no hint of this. The only warning sign will be when you contrast the conclusions of the model with your intuition and common sense. Unfortunately, in problems such as this, intuition is not foolproof. We should therefore watch out for hidden assumptions, which are implicit in the model formulation. We often think in terms of the model, and it may be hard to test these assumptions simply because they are taken for granted.
- Specifically relating to a state-space model of uncertainty, if you failed to include some states in the model, or defined the states too coarsely, ignoring some relevant sources of uncertainty, Bayesian updating will never be able to indicate this. Bayesian updating never

resurrects zeros – a state with zero probability a priori will also have a zero probability a posteriori. Similarly, a state that was not included in the analysis will never pop up due to Bayesian updating.

- The way you learn information may be informative in and of itself. Sometimes, the very fact that you know, or that you don't know, something tells you something new. In particular, we need to analyze people's incentives in sharing or not sharing information. For example, if your car battery has a warranty for five years, be careful in the sixth winter. If the producer is willing to give this warranty, you can interpret this as saying "This battery is most likely to work well for at least five years." It does not say that the battery will work well only five years; it says "at least five years." But, knowing the incentives of the producer, you can deduce that the battery may not last much longer than that. Put differently, if the battery were most likely to work well for, say, six years, the producer would be glad to signal this by a longer warranty period. From the fact that they didn't, you infer that six years are probably an exaggeration. Given the fact that a particular statement was made, rather than another that could have been made instead, you learn something that goes beyond the statement actually made.

Causality

The dialog in Problem 5.13 is about causality. Veronique argues, quite convincingly, that no matter what the competitors do, their firm should cut prices. In the language of game theory, cutting prices appears to be a *dominant strategy*. The problem with this analysis is that it assumes that this is a one-shot game, in which the choices of the players are independent of each other. These are indeed the circumstances in which the Prisoner's Dilemma, mentioned in the dialog, is rather compelling. But in real life price competition is not a one-shot game. A firm may cut prices on a given day, and wake up next morning to find that their competitors have also cut prices. And then they can react – and so can the competitors. Rather than a one-shot game, this would be better modeled as a repeated game.

Table 5.11 The competitor's response.

		Cut	Not Cut
The	A	Cut	Cut
competitor's	B	Cut	Not Cut
response	C	Not Cut	Cut
	D	Not Cut	Not Cut

In such a game, the choice of strategy of a player need not confine itself to a fixed move, such as a fixed level of prices. A strategy may react to the environment. In particular, the competitors may have chosen as their strategy a function, which determines whether to cut prices or not (tomorrow) based on our firm's decision (today).

Repeated game strategies therefore become rather complicated objects, allowing for all possible reactions, or all possible functions from history to moves in the future. It may seem that a full analysis of the repeated game is dauntingly complex. Moreover, in such an analysis you'll find so many strategies of the other player, each of which becomes a state of the world, that you may wonder how you are to assign probabilities to all of these.

But you don't have to fully analyze the entire repeated game in order to get the gist of the interaction. It suffices that you think of some states of the world in which the competitors do or do not cut prices *depending on* whether you do. In the simplest such model, you can consider two periods, and find that there are four states of the world (corresponding to four strategies of the opponent), rather than two. For each choice of yours, they can react by reducing prices or not. The four states can be generated as in Table 5.11.

Table 5.11 is not a decision matrix. This is a matrix which helps us define the states of the world, to be put in the decision matrix. When we do that, each row in Table 5.11, which may be thought of as a function from our choice Cut/Not Cut to their choice between the same options, will be one state of the world, that is, one column. The decision matrix may look as in Table 5.12.

Table 5.12   The competitor's strategy.

		Competitor's strategy			
		A	*B*	*C*	*D*
Our	Cut	L, L	L, L	L, H	L, H
choice	Not Cut	H, L	H, H	H, L	H, H

As an outcome, we introduce a pair of the letters L/H, standing for "low" and "high," respectively. The first letter designates our price, and the second the competitor's price. In the first row we choose to cut prices and our price is L, whereas in the second row we choose not to cut prices, resulting in a price H. In the first column, the competitor chooses to cut prices no matter what we do, and their price is L, while in the last, they do not cut prices, no matter what we do, and their price is H. But in columns B and C the competitor's strategy is responsive to ours: in B, for example, they cut prices only if we do, and thus we may end up with low prices for both (if we cut our price), or high prices for both (if we don't), and so on.

Veronique's analysis in the dialog implicitly assumes that the competitors do not react to our choice. This is tantamount to excluding strategies B and C, leaving only A (cut prices no matter what) and D (don't cut prices no matter what). In such a matrix it may indeed be true that we're better off cutting prices, and that this is our dominant strategy.

But this is no longer the case in the matrix in Table 5.12, which allows for the possibility of a responsive strategy on their part. In particular, there is a state of the world (strategy of the competitors) B, according to which both firms will end up with the same level of prices: low if we start a price war, and high if we don't. Once this state is in the matrix, the choice of cutting prices will no longer be a dominant strategy. In particular, if we put a non-negligible probability on this state, it may be wise not to start a price war. (There is also state C, which means that the competitors will cut prices only if we *don't*, but this state would probably deserve a lower probability.)

The point of this example is simple but extremely important: when you formulate your state space, you have to make sure that any possible causal relationships are reflected in the states. As in the previous problem, hidden assumptions that are introduced into the state space will not be corrected by Bayesian updating. In this case, the implicit assumption that the competitor's choice is causally independent of your own may be inadvertently introduced by failing to include several states of the world, and from that point on the analysis may be perfectly correct mathematically, but quite irrelevant to your problem.

We have discussed causality briefly in the chapter on consuming statistical data (Chapter 3). It is hard to establish causality, and often we will not have sufficient data to do so. But analysis of decision problems requires that we be aware of potential causal relationships, even if we end up assigning them low subjective probabilities.

The Sure Thing Principle

When we discussed the measurement of subjective probabilities we encountered a few difficulties. Specifically, when we measure subjective probability by the willingness to bet, some people prefer to bet on a fair coin than, say, on the stock market going up *as well as* on its going down; on the next US president being Republican *as well as* on the president being Democrat. These problems were illustrated in two famous thought experiments that Daniel Ellsberg published in 1961.[4] They are given in Problems 5.14 and 5.15. The former reads:

> There are two urns in front of you, each containing 100 balls. Urn A contains 50 red balls and 50 black balls. Urn B contains 100 balls, and you are told that each ball is either red or black, but you do not know how many of the 100 balls are red and how many are black.
>
> You are asked to choose an urn (A or B), and a color (red or black). Once you announce your choice, a ball will be drawn at random from the urn you named. If it is the color you named, you get $100. Otherwise you get nothing.

There are, therefore, four possible choices:

AR – betting on a red ball drawn out of urn A
AB – betting on a black ball drawn out of urn A
BR – betting on a red ball drawn out of urn B
BB – betting on a black ball drawn out of urn B

Almost all participants express indifference between AR and AB, as well as between BR and BB. Indeed, the information provided is completely symmetric, and there is no reason to prefer one to the other (within each of these pairs). However, not all participants are indifferent among all four choices. Many prefer each of the bets on the known urn (A) to each of the bets on the unknown urn (B).

Clearly, such preferences cannot be reconciled with the idea that your beliefs can be summarized by subjective probabilities that would govern your choice. The logic is precisely as in our analysis of Problems 5.1–5.10: urn A, the "known" urn, has probabilities 50%–50% of yielding a black vs. a red ball. It is supposed to be a fair chance device, comparable to a fair coin or a roulette wheel. By contrast, urn B generates outcomes with unknown probabilities. If you were to assign it your subjective probabilities, you will have to assign a probability to a red ball and a probability to a black ball that add up to 1. As a result, it is impossible that both these probabilities will be smaller than 50%. This example is very similar to Problems 5.4 and 5.9, as well as to 5.5 and 5.10. The important difference is that in the latter, there was no symmetry about the unknown event (such as the stock market going up or down). In Ellsberg's example the unknown probabilities relate to events that are completely symmetric, as far as we know.

At this point you may conclude that subjective probability is a nice tool, but that it may not always be applicable. Specifically, when probabilities are not known, it may be difficult to summarize our attitude to the problem by a single number. Indeed, the phenomenon that Ellsberg found in his experiments is that many people are *uncertainty averse*: other things being equal, they prefer known probabilities to unknown ones, or risk to uncertainty.[5,6] There is some evidence that uncertainty aversion, like risk aversion,

167

is much more common in the domain of gains than in the domain of losses, and that people may become uncertainty loving when it comes to losses, presumably due to the same effect of loss aversion discussed above in the context of risk.[7] Whether people like or dislike uncertainty in the domain of losses, many do not seem to behave in an uncertainty-neutral way, in the domains both of losses and of gains. Hence, subjective probabilities seem a little too restrictive. But before we draw this conclusion, we should say something about the arguments for summarizing beliefs by subjective probabilities.

In the case of expected utility theory under risk we briefly described von Neumann and Morgenstern's result, providing a serious argument in favor of expected utility maximization. There are similar arguments for subjective expected utility maximization in the context of uncertainty, that is, for the suggestion that you choose your subjective probability, and your utility function, and maximize the expectation of the utility with respect to the subjective probability. A description of these results is beyond the scope of this book.[8,9] But the second Ellsberg experiment gives us the gist of one important axiom.

Consider Problem 5.15:

> There is an urn containing 90 balls. Each ball can be red, blue, or yellow. You are also told that there are precisely 30 red balls in the urn. Hence, the remaining 60 balls are blue or yellow, but you don't know how many are blue and how many are yellow.
>
> A ball is to be drawn at random from the urn. You are offered choices between pairs of bets, where "betting on an event" implies winning $1,000 if the event occurs, and nothing otherwise:
>
> a. Betting on the ball being red
>   vs.
>   betting on the ball being blue
> b. [...]
> c. Betting on the ball being *not* red
>   vs.
>   betting on the ball being *not* blue
> d. [...]

Table 5.13   Red, blue, and yellow.

	Red	*Blue*	*Yellow*
Red	1,000	0	0
Blue	0	1,000	0
Not-Red	0	1,000	1,000
Not-Blue	1,000	0	1,000

Let us consider these bets given the state space. We may think of three states – "the ball drawn is red," which has a probability of 1/3, "the ball drawn is blue," and "the ball drawn is yellow," where we do not know how the last two share the overall probability of 2/3.

In Problem 5.15 you are asked to compare pairs of choices. If we put a few of them together, we may get the decision matrix in Table 5.13.

Many people express preferences for Red over Blue. The reason typically given is that, when you bet on red you know that your probability of winning the prize is 1/3, whereas when you bet on blue, the probability is unknown. It can be anywhere in the interval [0, 2/3], and while 1/3 is the mid-point of this interval, you do not know that this is indeed the probability of blue. In short, this is simply the intuition of uncertainty aversion.

Next consider Not-Red vs. Not-Blue. The same intuition would suggest that you prefer Not-Red, which yields the prize with a known probability of 2/3, to Not-Blue, which has a probability somewhere between 1/3 and 1.

But here comes the problem: if you consider Red and Blue, you notice that they both yield the same outcome, namely, zero, in the case a yellow ball is drawn. Hence, when you compare the two, you may ignore this state. It is as if you can assume that Yellow is known not to have occurred. If it does occur, the choice doesn't matter, so why not focus on the event over which the two bets differ?

This intuition is great, but we can make the same argument for the pair Not-Red and Not-Blue. They also yield the same payoff (this time, $1,000) in the case a yellow ball is drawn. Hence, we can ignore this event when we compare Not-Red and Not-Blue. The difficulty is that, if we ignore the Yellow column, "Red" becomes equivalent to "Not-Blue," and "Blue" equivalent to "Not-Red." That is, if you follow this line of reasoning, and you prefer Red to Blue, you should prefer Not-Blue to Not-Red, rather than vice versa.

The logic of this argument is basically an axiom suggested by Leonard Savage, typically referred to as the *Sure Thing Principle*. Roughly, it says that if two choices are equivalent given a certain event, we can assume that this event does not happen, and determine preferences between them based on its complement. It probably reminds you of the logic of the independence axiom of von Neumann and Morgenstern, though the models are somewhat different and the relationship between the two is not straightforward.

Historically, Ellsberg's experiments, from which we started, were designed to attack Savage's Sure Thing Principle. Descriptively, there is ample evidence that many people are indeed uncertainty averse. From a normative point of view decision theorists are divided on the question of whether the Sure Thing Principle can always be considered a necessary condition of rationality.

Those of you who violated the Sure Thing Principle in Problem 5.15 are asked to go over your choices again, and see if you would like to change them in light of this axiom. In fact, we could do a similar exercise in the case of Problem 5.14 (the two-urn experiment). In that problem we did not explicitly specify the state space, but if we were to do so, we could point out that uncertainty averse preferences in Problem 5.14 are also a violation of the Sure Thing Principle, and I could ask you to review your preferences in that case as well.

Some people who violate the Sure Thing Principle also insist on their preferences even after they are exposed to the axiom.[10] If we consider Problems 5.5 and 5.10 again, I may feel more comfortable with betting on a fair coin than on the party of the next president of the United States, even if you show me that, by so doing, I violate the axiom. In expressing such preferences, I may point out the difficulty that, with all due respect to the axiom, there is simply no way I can come up with a single number as my subjective probability of the next president being a Democrat. And then, given the choice between violating a very appealing axiom on the one hand, versus choosing a single probability number arbitrarily on the other, I may choose the former. It will probably not feel terribly good to know that I violate a nice axiom, but to make decisions as if I know probabilities that I do not know also doesn't feel very rational. This is a tough choice, and, as with all choices involving what's rational for us, this is a choice that depends on the decision maker and the problem at hand.

Alternative Models

In recent decades there has been a lot of theoretical interest in decision models that may serve as alternatives to subjective expected utility maximization. One such model that is relatively easy to explain is the maxmin model with "multiple priors."[11] The idea is that, rather than having a single probability for each event, as prescribed by the Bayesian model, the decision maker entertains a *set* of probability distributions. This idea is closer in spirit to the classical statistics mode of reasoning, where the problem is defined by a set of possible distributions, and, as opposed to the Bayesian approach, there is no quantification over these distributions. When it comes to making decisions, this model suggests that each decision is evaluated by its worst case expected utility. For example, suppose that my subjective probability of the next president of the United States being a Democrat is somewhere in the range [0.4, 0.6]. When offered a bet of $100 on a Democrat, I value it by

$$\text{Min}_{0.4 \le p \le 0.6} \left[p * u(\$100) + (1-p) * u(\$0) \right]$$
$$= 0.4 * u(\$100) + 0.6 * u(\$0)$$

And when offered a bet of $100 on a Republican, I value it by

$$\text{Min}_{0.4 \le p \le 0.6} \left[p * u(\$0) + (1-p) * u(\$100) \right]$$
$$= 0.4 * u(\$100) + 0.6 * u(\$0)$$

Thus, both can be strictly lower than the value of a bet on (either side of) a fair coin. According to this theory, uncertainty aversion is built into the decision making process, since each alternative is evaluated by the probability that results in the worst case for this alternative.

Models such as the maxmin expected utility have been used to explain a number of phenomena in finance and economics. One example is the "home bias," referring to the observed phenomenon that traders appear to prefer to trade stocks of their own countries, rather than to trade overseas.[12] The comparison of a domestic and a foreign asset is arguably reminiscent of Ellsberg's two-urn experiment: the domestic asset is more familiar, and more is known about its probability distribution, as compared with the foreign asset. Hence, the urn with the known probabilities may be thought of as an idealized domestic asset, whereas the urn with the unknown probabilities corresponds to the foreign asset. The preferences observed in laboratory experiments, where many people prefer to bet on the known probabilities rather than the unknown ones, are consistent with the real-life phenomenon that people prefer trading "known," domestic assets to trading "unknown," foreign ones.

Objective Probabilities

Problems 5.16 and 5.17 are supposed to remind us that not all probabilities are subjective. They read as follows.

Problem 5.16

Suppose that I am about to undergo a medical operation. I ask my doctor what the probability of success is. How can my doctor provide me with an objective answer?

Problem 5.17

Suppose that I'm interested in an investment whose value depends on the possibility of war. I consult an expert on international relations, and ask him what the probability of war in the Middle East in the next year is. How can the expert provide an objective answer?

These problems are challenging because they deal with unique events: in the medical example, no two patients are the same. In the international relations example, no two situations of conflict are the same. Hence, the notion of objective probability as the empirical frequency in a large database doesn't quite apply. If I were the patient in Problem 5.16, I would not wish to base my decision simply on the relative frequencies, because the other patients may differ from me in terms of medically relevant variables such as age, gender, weight, and so on. Similarly, considering the investment in Problem 5.17, it seems silly to assume that the probability of war is just the relative frequency of past wars. Indeed, the relative frequency may not even be well defined in such an example: will it cover all of recorded history, or only recent decades? Will it be limited to the region in question, or include similar ones? In short, the simple notion of relative frequencies does not provide a good definition of probability in either of these examples.

And yet, these examples are given here to remind us that sometimes objective probabilities can be defined even when simple empirical frequencies cannot be used. How such probabilities are defined statistically is beyond the scope of this book. But you should be asking yourself what type of answer you might expect, and how you can use it.

In the case of the medical example, there are large databases on medical procedures, and sophisticated statistical techniques to try to estimate probabilities for each given patient. Statisticians, as well as medical doctors, may be wrong, and the publication of new studies may change their minds. But the probabilistic assessments they provide are often objective in the sense that they do not depend on the subjective views of the physician or the statistician.

The case of the probability of war (in Problem 5.17) is different. In cases such as this we sometimes get probabilistic assessments, but these tend to be the expert's subjective probability, rather than an objective probability that the expert has computed. In other words, if you ask a different expert about the probability of war, you should not be surprised to find a very different assessment. For that reason, many international relations experts would be reluctant to quantify their beliefs in a probabilistic manner.

What is the difference between these two domains? While in both of them we have many observations that are very different from each other, in the medical example these observations are, for the most part, causally independent. This fact allows experts to employ sophisticated statistical techniques, dealing with the dissimilarities among the observations and attempting to assess the way that probabilities vary with respect to these dissimilarities. But in the case of war, as in the case of a major economic crisis, past observations are not only different in many parameters; they are also causally related, to each other as well as to the case at hand. As a result, there is much more room for a variety of causal theories, and for subjective beliefs in them, at the expense of statistical techniques that can be viewed as objective.

Exercises

1. Consider the following two questions:
    a. Which is more likely: to observe snow tomorrow or to observe two consecutive tosses of a fair coin coming up Head?

    _____

    _____

    b. Which is more likely: to observe no precipitation tomorrow or to observe a roulette wheel coming up on a number that is different than 7?

    _____

    _____

Which combinations of answers to (a) and (b) are consistent with beliefs that can be represented by subjective probabilities?

_____

_____

2. Consider the following two questions:
   a. Which is more likely: that the DJIA will be above its current level two months hence, or that a fair coin comes up Head?

   _____

   _____

   b. Which is more likely: that the DJIA will be below its current level two months hence, or that a fair coin comes up Head?

   _____

   _____

   Which combinations of answers to (a) and (b) are consistent with beliefs that can be represented by subjective probabilities?

   _____

   _____

3. Ann thinks that a Democrat and a Republican are just as likely to win the upcoming US elections. She prefers to bet on either of them winning than on a fair coin coming up Head. What can you say about Ann?
   a. She behaves like the majority of participants in the Ellsberg experiments.
   b. Based on this information alone, she will probably prefer to buy a local equity rather than a foreign one.
   c. Based on this information alone, she will probably prefer to buy a foreign equity rather than a local one.

d. She will be comfortable with a Bayesian model describing her beliefs.

_____

_____

_____

4. Assessing the probability that the globe will warm up by more than 3° (Celsius) is a big challenge. Explain why, and what is the difference between this and assessing the probability that a 50-year-old man will develop heart disease over the next ten years.

_____

_____

_____

Notes

1 This is implicit in his writings, as opposed to Daniel Bernoulli's suggestion of expected utility maximization in the context of risk. But if we recall that Pascal was the person who invented the concept of expectation in probability theory, there is little doubt that this is the type of calculation his text refers to.

2 Dreze, J. H. (1961) Les fondements logiques de l'utilite cardinale et de la probabilite subjective. *La Decision.* Colloques Internationaux du CNRS; Karni, E., Schmeidler, D. and Vind, K. (1983) On state dependent preferences and subjective probabilities. *Econometrica,* 51, 1021–1031; Karni, E. (1985) *Decision Making Under Uncertainty: The Case of State Dependent Preferences.* Harvard University Press.

3 The fact that the Monty Hall example is more than an amusement and relates to this general point was made by Roger Myerson.

4 Ellsberg, D. (1961) Risk, ambiguity and the Savage axioms. *Quarterly Journal of Economics,* 75, 643–669.

The term "uncertainty," as opposed to "risk," was used by Knight. Ellsberg used the term "ambiguity." "Ambiguity aversion" and "uncertainty aversion" are synonymous, and both are used today.

5 Ellsberg did not run laboratory experiments; he used questionnaires addressed to experts in the field. But his findings have since been replicated by many carefully run experiments.

6 Knight, F. H. (1921) *Risk, Uncertainty, and Profit*. Houghton Mifflin.

7 Dobbs, I. M. (1991) A Bayesian approach to decision-making under ambiguity. *Economica*, 58, 417–440.

8 Building on earlier work by Frank Ramsey, Bruno de Finetti, and von Neumann and Morgenstern, Leonard Savage provided, in 1954, a very compelling axiomatic argument for subjective expected utility maximization.

9 Ramsey, F. P. (1931) Truth and probability, in *The Foundation of Mathematics and Other Logical Essays*. Routledge and Kegan Paul, pp. 156–198. Reprinted in Kyburg, H. E., Jr & Smokler, H. E. (eds) (1964) *Studies in Subjective Probability*. John Wiley & Sons, Inc., pp. 61–92 (2nd edn 1980, Krieger); de Finetti, B. (1937) La prevision: ses lois logiques, ses sources subjectives. *Annales de l'Institut Henri Poincare*, 7, 1–68; Savage, L. J. (1954) *The Foundations of Statistics*. John Wiley & Sons, Inc. (2nd edn 1972, Dover).

10 Slovic, P. & Tversky, A. (1974) Who accepts Savage's axiom? *Behavioral Science*, 19, 368–373.

11 Gilboa, I. and Schmeidler, D. (1989) Maxmin expected utility with a non-unique prior. *Journal of Mathematical Economics*, 18, 141–153.

12 French, K. and Poterba, J. (1991) Investor diversification and international equity markets. *American Economic Review*, 81, 222–226; Epstein, L. G. and Miao, J. (2003) A two-person dynamic equilibrium under ambiguity. *Journal of Economic Dynamics and Control*, 27, 1253–1288.

6

Well-Being and Happiness

Introduction

Are you happy? What should happen to make you happy ten years hence? Are people around you happy? What determines their happiness? And is there any reason to worry about these questions?

Some people might think that these are not questions that should be discussed in a book such as this, and that they should not concern management and economics students. Presumably, readers of this book are concerned about making better decisions, making more money or fewer investment mistakes, and they are not interested in discussions about happiness or the meaning of life. But in recent years there has been a growing understanding that these questions are relevant, from both a descriptive and a normative point of view.

Descriptively, we wish to understand the behavior of others without necessarily attempting to change it. And for this purpose it's important to know what motivates people and what they define as their well-being. Normatively, each of us may stop to think what we seek in life, now and in the future. If we very effectively pursue the wrong goal, we will hardly be making good decisions.

Making Better Decisions, by Itzhak Gilboa © 2011 John Wiley & Sons, Inc.

I therefore devote this chapter to the questions of happiness and well-being. It is a shorter chapter than the others, because I believe that scientific knowledge is more limited in this domain, and we will be left with more question marks than usual. Still, I hope that the questions will be worth thinking about.

Problems – Group A

Problem 6.1

Mary works in your public relations office. She is doing a good job and you're pleased with her performance. About six months ago, she hired a new employee, named Jane, who turned out to be a born talent. They get along fine.

Mary's direct boss just quit, and you're looking for someone for the job. You don't think that Mary is perfect for it. By contrast, Jane seems a great fit. But it may be awkward to promote Jane and make Mary her subordinate. A colleague suggested that you go ahead and do this, but give both of them a nice raise to solve the problem.

What percentage of a salary raise do you think will solve the problem?

_____

_____

Problem 6.2

As we're nearing the end of this book, it is time to get some feedback. Please answer the following questions:

1. Did you find the explanations clear?   Yes_____   No_____
2. Did you find the topics interesting?   Yes_____   No_____
3. Did you find the graphs well done?   Yes_____   No_____
4. On a scale of 0–10, your overall evaluation for the book is:

_____

_____

Problem 6.3

Robert and John went to school together, and they got married at roughly the same time. They lived in the city and enjoyed it very much.

Robert and his wife have not had any children. John and his wife had a first child after one year, and, two years later, they had a second one, now eight months old. As a result, John had to move to the suburbs, took a mortgage to buy a large house and feels financially strained.

Robert is on a ski vacation with his wife, while John is at home. He can't even dream of a ski vacation with the two children, to say nothing of the expense. In fact, John would be quite happy just to have a good night's sleep.

Do you think that Robert is happier than John?

_____

_____

Problems – Group B

Problem 6.4

Mary works in your public relations office. She is doing a good job and you're pleased with her performance. About six months ago, she hired a new employee, named Jane, who turned out to be a born talent. They get along fine.

Mary's direct boss just quit, and you're looking for someone for the job. You don't think that Mary is perfect for it. By contrast, Jane seems a great fit. But it may be awkward to promote Jane and make Mary her subordinate. A colleague suggested that you go ahead and do this, but give both of them a nice raise to solve the problem.

What percentage of a salary raise do you think will solve the problem?

_____

_____

Problem 6.5

As we're nearing the end of this book, it is time to get some feedback. Please answer the following questions:

1. On a scale of 0–10, your overall evaluation for the book is:
2. Did you find the explanations clear?   Yes_____   No_____
3. Did you find the topics interesting?   Yes_____   No_____
4. Did you find the graphs well done?   Yes_____   No_____

_____

_____

Problem 6.6

Robert and John went to school together, and they got married at roughly the same time. They lived in the city and enjoyed it very much.

Robert and his wife have not had any children. John and his wife had a first child after one year, and, two years later, they had a second one, now eight months old. As a result, John had to move to the suburbs, took a mortgage to buy a large house and feels financially strained.

Robert is on a ski vacation with his wife, while John is at home. He can't even dream of a ski vacation with the two children, to say nothing of the expense. In fact, John would be quite happy just to have a good night's sleep.

Do you think that Robert is happier than John?

_____

_____

Well-Being

Problems 6.1 and 6.4 were identical, and they read:

Mary works in your public relations office. She is doing a good job and you're pleased with her performance. About six months ago, she hired a new employee, named Jane, who turned out to be a born talent. They get along fine.

Mary's direct boss just quit, and you're looking for someone for the job. You don't think that Mary is perfect for it. By contrast, Jane seems a great fit. But it may be awkward to promote Jane and make Mary her subordinate. A colleague suggested that you go ahead and do this, but give both of them a nice raise to solve the problem.

What percentage of a salary raise do you think will solve the problem?

We obviously don't know Mary and her personality. Maybe envy is very foreign to her, and maybe she has no ambition to be promoted. Maybe she shares your admiration for Jane's talent and it wouldn't even cross her mind that she, rather than her subordinate, could have gotten her boss's job. But it is also quite possible that Mary would feel upset. It's not nice to see one's subordinate being promoted faster than oneself, and it can be outright humiliating to report to someone who only recently reported to you. In fact, your intuition might tell you that no salary raise will be able to solve the problem. In many institutions, appointing Jane to the job would be a taboo, something that you would do only if you actually wished Mary to leave. If you would indeed like Mary to stay and remain a dedicated employee, you may have to promote Jane to a job in another department, or find another job for Mary, or do something else that would avoid negative emotions on Mary's part.

Envy is not an emotion we are very proud of. It is one of the seven deadly sins. And yet, it is very human. (If it were not, perhaps it would not have deserved so much attention.) People are very sensitive to their social status, and this seems to be common to other species as well. Within economics, James Duesenberry suggested (in 1949) the "relative income hypothesis," according to which people attempt to maximize their relative standing in the income distribution, rather than income itself.[1] Having more money, but being at a lower social rank, may be worse than having less money but a higher social rank.

Can we abolish envy, and perhaps also other emotions that we tend to frown upon? This is not an easy question. Each of us may try, at the very least, not to act on such emotions, and if possible also not to show them. Using cognitive techniques, we can also try not to experience these emotions, or at least to experience them less often. But it is not obvious that we can decide to stop envying people and indeed succeed in this task. And even if we do, it would be imprudent to assume that everyone else has also abolished envy.

Envy and social status are just two examples of non-material factors of *well-being*. It seems very obvious that people care not only about money, or what money can buy, but also about friendship and love, self-fulfillment and satisfaction, leisure and peace of mind. The fact that well-being is not synonymous with money has been understood for several millennia. There is hardly a human culture that has not made this point. From ancient philosophical and religious teachings to recent Hollywood movies, we learn that "money isn't everything," "money doesn't buy happiness," and so forth.

In recent decades, scientific studies in the social sciences have attempted to document the relationship between money and well-being. Researchers such as Richard Easterlin and Ed Diener have measured well-being, typically by a person's self-report, and studied how it changes with various factors.[2] This measure, called *subjective well-being*, has been found to be significantly correlated with income, but not to a large degree (with a correlation coefficient around 0.2).[3] Easterlin found that the correlation was higher within a given cohort than across cohorts. His explanation was that subjective well-being depends not only on income, but also on the relationship between one's income and one's aspiration level for income, and the latter is determined, to a large extent, by comparisons to others. Within a cohort, people tend to compare themselves with the same group, and therefore to have a similar aspiration level. This results in a relatively high correlation between income and reported well-being. But across cohorts, when we compare people in different age groups, the older, who tend to be richer, also have richer friends. Therefore their aspiration levels are higher than those of the younger. Consequently, reported well-being need not increase with age even though income does.

The notion of an aspiration level that adapts as a result of experiences might remind you of "adaptation level theory," by Harry Helson, mentioned in Chapter 4 (in the context of prospect theory).[4] Indeed, followers of Helson applied his theory, which focuses on sensual perception, to the question of well-being. In a famous study from 1978, Brickman, Coates, and Janoff-Bulman compared the reported well-being of individuals who underwent very dramatic positive and negative events: people who won lotteries on the one hand, and people who became handicapped due to an accident on the other. The striking finding was that, after a while, the reported well-being seemed to be the same in the two groups.[5] Philip Brickman and Donald Campbell pushed this idea further,[6] arguing that there is no point in improving people's material conditions, since they anyway adapt to the new circumstances. According to them, human beings were like little rodents running on a "hedonic treadmill": the faster we run, the faster we need to keep running to feel content. Happiness, they argued, will not be achieved this way.

Measurement Issues

This dramatic conclusion by Brickman and Campbell seemed suspicious to many people. Economists, in particular, are used to thinking of utility according to the *revealed preference* paradigm: we first observe people's choices, and then we assign to them, as outside observers, a function that can describe their choices. "Having a higher utility," according to this paradigm, simply means "Will be chosen, given the opportunity." Based on this thinking, economists who hear about the lottery winners and the handicapped people having the same reported well-being ask, "Yes, but would the lottery winners like to trade places?"

This raises a more general question: what exactly is being measured by subjective well-being? How much can we trust the answer we get to guide our decisions, whether as individuals or as societies, regarding ourselves and regarding others? These questions become more relevant in light of psychological studies that showed that reported well-being can be manipulated in various ways. To see an example, let us contrast Problem 6.2 and Problem 6.5. The first reads:

Problem 6.2

As we're nearing the end of this book, it is time to get some feedback. Please answer the following questions:

1. Did you find the explanations clear?   Yes_____   No_____
2. Did you find the topics interesting?   Yes_____   No_____
3. Did you find the graphs well done?   Yes_____   No_____
4. On a scale of 0–10, your overall evaluation for the book is:

Whereas the second (6.5) has the same questions in a slightly different order: no. (4) (the one about overall evaluation) is asked first.

We would like to focus on the correlation between the answers to items (3) and (4) in Problem 6.2, and items (1) and (4) in Problem 6.5: the satisfaction with the graphs in the book, and the overall evaluation. It makes sense that there will be a positive correlation between them: other things being equal, the more satisfied you are with the graphs, the more satisfied you'd be with the book as a whole. That is, we should find a higher average satisfaction among the people who marked "yes" for the graphs question than among those who marked "no." The point is that this correlation may differ between the two problems. A typical finding would be that this correlation is higher in 6.2 than in 6.5.

The reason seems obvious: in 6.2, just before you're asked about the overall evaluation, the issue of the graphs is being brought to your attention. You are asked to focus on it, and whatever you think about the graphs, good or bad, is likely to affect your overall evaluation. By contrast, in 6.5 you're first asked about the overall evaluation, and, if you don't go back to revise your answer, the quality of the graphs is likely to play a more minor role in determining this evaluation than when you were asked to first focus on this effect.

Similar phenomena exist when people are asked to report their well-being, or "satisfaction with life as a whole." The latter concept is quite vague, and by focusing your attention on certain aspects of your life rather than others, one can manipulate your responses.[7] As a result, it is not obvious that subjective well-being is a robust enough measure to base decisions upon.

Difficulties of this type were part of the motivation for Daniel Kahneman and his colleagues to think about other ways to measure well-being. Kahneman has also shown that the way individuals recall events can be very different from the way they experience them when they unfold. He promotes the view that (i) well-being should be measured as the sum, over time points, of the instantaneous utility; and (ii) this instantaneous utility is best measured objectively, according to the judgment of others. Specifically, Kahneman and his colleagues suggest the Day Reconstruction Method (DRM),[8] according to which individuals recall their experiences of a day, hour by hour, these experiences are independently ranked for pleasurability, and well-being is measured as the sum of these pleasurability rankings.

What's Happiness?

Consider Problems 6.3 and 6.6, which were identical. They read:

> Robert and John went to school together, and they got married at roughly the same time. They lived in the city and enjoyed it very much.
>
> Robert and his wife have not had any children. John and his wife had a first child after one year, and, two years later, they had a second one, now eight months old. As a result, John had to move to the suburbs, took a mortgage to buy a large house and feels financially strained.
>
> Robert is on a ski vacation with his wife, while John is at home. He can't even dream of a ski vacation with the two children, to say nothing of the expense. In fact, John would be quite happy just to have a good night's sleep.
>
> Do you think that Robert is happier than John?

Of course, this is not the type of question to which you expect a correct answer. We do not know who is happier, and it's not even clear what the meaning of this question is. The point of the problem, however, is to question our measurement of well-being. If we use subjective well-being questionnaires, we may find Robert saying that he's quite content with his life, whereas John might complain about financial stress, sleep deprivation, and scarcity of leisure. Indeed, studies of subjective well-being find that people without children report a higher well-being than people with children, roughly throughout the parenting period.[9] If we were to resort to the Day Reconstruction Method, we would probably find that Robert spends much more of his time sleeping, going out, and having ski vacations than does John, whose time is devoted to changing diapers and spending sleepless nights with a screaming baby. Independent observers would surely rank "taking a ski vacation" as much more pleasurable than "trying to put a screaming baby to bed." As a result, both methods might indicate that it's a silly idea to have children.

But this conclusion doesn't make sense. First, if we take the economists' revealed preferences approach, having children can't be such a bad idea if so many people consciously choose to do so generation after generation. Second, if we talk to parents, they will often say that their children are the source of their happiness, the meaning of their lives, and so forth. While it may be very hard to measure this happiness, it seems intuitive that a hug one gets from one's child at the end of a work day can change one's experience during that day. To state the obvious, this does not mean that you have to have children in order to be happy. Moreover, it is quite possible that people who chose to have children have managed to convince themselves, perhaps with the help of society, that they are happy. The point is that some factors, which appear very important to people's happiness, may not be fully captured by existing measures of well-being.

Where does this leave us? We have a significant body of research on well-being, and we can use it to remind ourselves that money should not be equated with happiness. This is important for us to know when we are dealing with others (such as employees as in Problems 6.1 and 6.4), as well as when we plan our own lives. But scientific knowledge is far from providing a clear answer to the question of what well-being is, let alone of what happiness is. The attempts to measure these concepts may well suggest that the question is ill-defined.

We have mentioned that psychology distinguishes between positive and negative experiences, as reflected in the gain–loss asymmetry discussed in prospect theory. It appears that the measurement of well-being is another case in which the negative range differs from the positive one: while it is not clear what happiness is, it is much clearer what misery is. We may not be able to agree whether a person is happy thanks to being healthy, free, and wealthy; but we will tend to agree that people who are sick, imprisoned, or starving are unhappy.

Throughout this book I have been emphasizing the view that it is up to you to determine what a good decision is for you. Clearly, this subjective approach also applies to the questions of well-being and happiness. Our goal here is to raise the questions rather than to provide the answers.

Exercises

1. An employee had to choose between two payment schemes for a three-year contract. The first offered $90,000 in the first year, $100,000 in the second, and $110,000 in the third, while the second offered the same amounts in the opposite order (starting from $110,000 in the first year and going down to $90,000). The employee chose the former.
   a. Why does this choice contradict classical economic theory?
   b. How would you explain such a choice?

   _____

   _____

   _____

2. Suppose that a newly developed drug improves mood with absolutely no side effects, in either the short or the long term. The drug is not expensive to produce.
   a. Would you recommend that it be administered to the entire population?

b. Would you like to take it yourself if people around you do not?

_____

_____

_____

3. Lack of sunlight has been found to contribute to depression among some people. One solution is the introduction of artificial substitutes for sunlight, which were proven to reduce depressive symptoms. Would you recommend using such substitutes? Compare your answer to this question with your answer to question (2).

_____

_____

_____

4. Assume that people's well-being is affected by their aspiration level, where the latter is determined by the average performance of people they think of as their peers. Suppose that globalization is only reflected in an increased flow of information among people around the globe. How will it affect well-being?

_____

_____

_____

Notes

1 Duesenberry, J. S. (1949) *Income, Saving, and the Theory of Consumer Behavior*. Harvard University Press.
2 Easterlin, R. (1973) Does money buy happiness? *The Public Interest*, 30, 3–10; Easterlin, R. A. (1974) Does economic growth improve the human lot? Some empirical evidence, in *Nations and Households in Economic*

Growth (eds P. A. David and M. W. Reder). Academic Press, pp. 89–125; Diener, E. (1984) Subjective well-being. *Psychological Bulletin*, 95, 542–575. However, see also Lucas, R. E., Dyrenforth, P. S. and Diener, E. (2008) Four myths about subjective well-being. *Social and Personality Compass*, 2, 2001–2015.

3   Easterlin (1974), see note 2.

4   Helson, H. (1947) Adaptation-level as frame of reference for prediction of psychophysical data. *American Journal of Psychology*, 60, 1–29; Helson, H. (1948) Adaptation-level as a basis for a quantitative theory of frames of reference. *Psychological Review*, 55, 297–313; Helson, H. (1964) *Adaptation Level Theory: An Experimental and Systematic Approach to Behavior*. Harper and Row.

5   Brickman, P., Coates, D. and Janoff-Bulman, R. (1978) Lottery winners and accident victims: is happiness relative? *Journal of Personality and Social Psychology*, 36, 917–927.

6   Brickman, P. and Campbell, D. T. (1971) Hedonic relativism and planning the good society, in *Adaptation Level Theory: A Symposium* (ed. M. H. Appley). Academic Press, pp. 287–304.

7   Strack, F., Martin, L. and Schwarz, N. (1988) Priming and communication: social determinants of information use in judgments of life satisfaction. *European Journal of Social Psychology*, 18, 429–442; Schwarz, N. and Clore, G. L. (1983) Mood, misattribution, and judgments of well-being: informative and directive functions of affective states. *Journal of Personality and Social Psychology*, 45, 513–523.

8   Kahneman, D., Krueger, A. B., Schkade, D. A., Schwarz, N. and Stone, A. A. (2004) A survey method for characterizing daily life experience: the Day Reconstruction Method. *Science*, 306, 1776–1780.

9   Mcklanahan, S. and Adams, J. (1987) Parenthood and psychological well-being. *Annual Review of Sociology*, 13, 237–257; Umberson, D. and Gove, W. R. (1989) Parenthood and psychological well-being: theory, measurement, and stage in family life course. *Journal of Family Issues*, 10, 440–462.

Appendix A

Optimal Choice[1]

A fundamental of optimal choice theory is the distinction between feasibility and desirability. A choice is *feasible* if it is possible for the decision maker, that is, one of the things that she *can* do. An outcome is *desirable* if the decision maker wishes to bring it about. Typically, feasibility is considered to be a dichotomous concept, while desirability is continuous: a choice is either feasible or not, with no shades in between; by contrast, an outcome is desirable to a certain degree, and different outcomes can be ranked according to their desirability.

We typically assume that desirability is measured by a *utility function u*, such that the higher the utility of a choice, the better will the decision maker like it. This might appear odd, as many people do not know what functions are and almost no one can be observed walking around with a calculator and finding the alternative with the highest utility. But it turns out that very mild assumptions on choice are sufficient to determine that the decision maker behaves *as if* she had a utility function that she was attempting to maximize. If the number of choices is finite, the assumptions are the following:

1. Completeness: for every two choices, the decision maker can say that she prefers the first to the second, the second to the first, or that she is indifferent between them.

Making Better Decisions, by Itzhak Gilboa © 2011 John Wiley & Sons, Inc.

2. Transitivity: for every three choices *a, b, c*, if *a* is at least as good as *b*, and *b* is at least as good as *c*, then *a* is at least as good as *c*.

It turns out that these assumptions are equivalent to the claim that there exists a function *u* such that, for every two alternatives *a* and *b*, *a* is at least as good as *b* if and only if $u(a) \geq u(b)$. Descriptively, this means that anyone who behaves in accordance with the two axioms above can be thought of as a utility maximizer for an appropriately chosen utility function (reflecting the person's tastes). This is true of people whose mental processes may be very different from maximization of anything. From a normative point of view, the implication is that if one likes to satisfy the two axioms above, then one may do so by choosing a utility function and making sure that one always chooses the alternative with the highest utility. Any other algorithm that guarantees adherence to these axioms has to be equivalent to maximization of a certain function, and therefore the decision maker might well specify the function explicitly.

When we consider choice under certainty, there is no need to distinguish between choices and outcomes: the decision maker knows that a given choice leads to a particular outcome. If, however, uncertainty is present, the decision maker may choose an *act*, but she does not know which *outcome* will result from this act. In this case we introduce *states of nature* or *states of the world*.[2] Given the decision maker's choice of an act, and nature's choice of a state, the outcome is determined. Thus, the decision maker has feasible acts, she faces possible states of nature, and she will experience outcomes that are more or less desirable to her.

For a simple example of optimal choice under certainty, consider the consumer's problem. The consumer has income *I* and there are *n* products in the market. Product *i* costs p_i per unit. The consumer can decide what quantity $x_i \geq 0$ they will buy of each product, thereby choosing a *bundle* $(x_1, x_2, \ldots, x_n)$. The feasibility constraint is that the bundle be affordable, that is, it has to satisfy the *budget constraint*:

$$p_1 x_1 + p_2 x_2 + ... + p_n x_n \leq I$$

and desirability is measured by a utility function u. Thus, for each bundle $(x_1, x_2, ..., x_n)$, $u(x_1, x_2, ..., x_n)$ is a number that measures its desirability. The higher is the value of the function u, the more desirable is the bundle, and the more pleased is the consumer.

For our purposes, it is worthwhile highlighting what this model does not include. Choices are given as quantities of products. Various descriptions of the products, which may be part of their frames, are not part of the discussion. The utility function measures desirability on a scale. We did not mention any special point on this scale, such as a reference point. Further, choices are bundles of products to be consumed by the consumer in question at the time of the problem. They do not allow us to treat a certain bundle differently based on the consumer's history of consumption, or on the consumption of others around them. Hence, the very language of the model assumes that the consumer does not care what others have, they feel no envy, nor any disappointment in the case when their income drops as compared with last period, and so on.

It is important to emphasize that the general paradigm of rational choice does not necessitate these constraints. For instance, instead of the n products the consumer can consume today, we may have a model with $2n$ products, reflecting their consumption today and their consumption yesterday. This would allow us to specify a utility function u that takes into account considerations such as aspiration levels, disappointment, and so forth. Or, we can use more variables to indicate the average consumption in the consumer's social group, and then the utility function can capture social considerations such as the consumer's ranking in society and so forth. Indeed, such models have been suggested in the past[3] and have become more popular with the rise of behavioral economics. These models show that the *paradigm* of rational choice is rather flexible. Yet, the specific *theory* of consumer behavior which is dominant in economics restricts the relevant variables to be independent of history, others' experiences, emotions, and other factors which might be among the determinants of well-being.

Notes

1 The two appendices contain but the very minimum required to make the discussion in the text intelligible. Because they are no more than a collection of definitions and fact sheets, readers who have never seen this material at all are advised to consult a standard textbook.
2 These two terms are not completely synonymous, but for our purposes they can be used interchangeably.
3 Duesenberry, J. S. (1949) *Income, Saving, and the Theory of Consumer Behavior*. Harvard University Press.

Appendix B

Probability and Statistics

The basic probability model starts with a list of all that can happen, that is, of the *states of nature*. Assume that the states are $s_1, s_2, ..., s_n$. Each state is considered to be a complete specification of all that matters to the decision maker. An *event* is a collection (set) of states. Thus, an event is simply something that may or may not happen, and in our natural language it corresponds to a proposition, a statement that may be true or false. For every state s_i there is an event that corresponds to that state alone, $\{s_i\}$, but events may have more than one state in them.

Assume, for example, that we are about to roll a die. The relevant states are $\{1, 2, 3, 4, 5, 6\}$ corresponding to the side of the die that comes up. An event can be $\{2\}$, that is, the die comes up on 2, but also $\{1, 2, 3, 4\}$, which stands for "the number that comes up is less than 5," or $\{1, 3, 5\}$, "the number is odd," and so forth. We can also define the sure event, S, and the impossible event, Ø.

We perform operations on events, which correspond to the logical operations of conjunction, disjunction, and negation, corresponding to "and," "or," and "not," respectively. When applied to events, we call these operations *intersection, union,* and *complement,* and they are denoted by the symbols ∩, ∪, and ¬, respectively.

Making Better Decisions, by Itzhak Gilboa © 2011 John Wiley & Sons, Inc.

You may verify that the following properties hold for any two events A, B:

$$A \cup S = S \quad A \cap S = A$$
$$A \cup \varnothing = A \quad A \cap \varnothing = \varnothing$$
$$\neg(A \cup B) = \neg A \cap \neg B$$
$$\neg(A \cap B) = \neg A \cup \neg B$$

A *probability* is a function, assigning non-negative numbers to events, attempting to measure their plausibility. Thus, if A is an event, we wish $P(A) \geq 0$ to measure how likely it is to happen. It is a convention that the probability of the sure event is 1, that is, that $P(S) = 1$. When we think of events that may or may not occur in each of repeated identical trials, we can define $P(A)$ to be the *empirical relative frequency* of A, namely, the proportion of the trials in which A occurred relative to the entire number of trials.

If we take this *frequentist* interpretation of probability, we will find out that, for any two events A and B,

$$P(A) + P(B) = P(A \cap B) + P(A \cup B)$$

Hence this condition is considered to be part of the definition of probability in general. It can be verified that it is equivalent to the (seemingly weaker) condition that

$$P(A) + P(B) = P(A \cup B)$$
whenever $A \cap B = \varnothing$

that is, if we consider two *disjoint* events, that can never co-occur ($A \cap B = \varnothing$) the probability of their union (one of them occurring) should be the same as the sum of their probabilities.

It follows that, for every event A,

$$P(A) + P(\neg A) = 1$$

because A and not-A ($\neg A$) are two disjoint events whose union is S, and the probability of S is 1.

The notion of *conditional* probability attempts to capture the way that beliefs change as a result of receiving new information. If we learn that event B has occurred, and I ask myself how likely A is to occur, I should first realize that A can only occur if the intersection A ∩ B occurs, because B is already a given fact. Thus, I should base my answer on the probability of this intersection, $P(A \cap B)$. Since we have the convention that the probability of the sure event is 1, we want to make sure that if I substitute S for A I get 1. But $P(S \cap B) = P(B)$ need not be 1. So we re-normalize by dividing the probability of the intersection by the probability of the known event. This leads to Bayes's definition of conditional probability: the conditional probability of A given B is

$$P(A \mid B) = P(A \cap B) / P(B)$$

This also means that

$$P(A \cap B) = P(B) * P(A \mid B)$$

In other words: one way to find the probability that both A and B occur is to consider first the probability that B occurs, and then to multiply it by the *conditional* probability that A occurs once we know that B is already the case.

Two events are *independent* if they do not convey information about each other. We define A to be independent of B if

$$P(A \mid B) = P(A)$$

that is, if your beliefs about A before and after learning B are the same. If A is independent of B, B is also independent of A, and we have (assuming all numbers are positive)

$$P(B \mid A) = P(B)$$

and

$$P(A \cap B) = P(A) * P(B)$$

We also make use of the following fact: the probability of an event A can be split according to another event B:

$$P(A) = P(A \cap B) + P(A \cap \neg B)$$

because the two subevents, (A ∩ B) and (A ∩ ~B), are disjoint (cannot happen together), and together they make up all of A. If we now proceed to write the probability of each of these intersections as the product of the probability of the one event (first B, then ~B) multiplied by the probability of A given that event, we get

$$P(A) = P(A \cap B) + P(A \cap \neg B)$$
$$= P(B)^* P(A \mid B) + P(\neg B)^* P(A \mid \neg B)$$

Recall that the probabilities of B and of not-B have to sum up to 1. Thus, if we have

$$\beta = P(B)$$

and

$$1 - \beta = P(\neg B)$$

we obtain

$$P(A) - \beta^* P(A \mid B) + (1 \quad \beta)^* P(A \mid \neg B)$$

which says that the probability of A is a weighted average of the probability of A given B and the probability of A given not-B, where the weights are the probabilities of B and not-B, respectively. This means that $P(A)$ is always in between these two conditional probabilities: if

$$P(A \mid B) > P(A \mid \neg B)$$

then

$$P(A \mid B) > P(A) > P(A \mid \neg B)$$

and vice versa: if $P(A \mid B) < P(A \mid \neg B)$ then $P(A \mid B) < P(A) < P(A \mid \neg B)$. In the case where A and B are independent, all these inequalities become equalities.

Clearly, this is symmetric: we can also write

$$P(B) = P(B \cap A) + P(B \cap \neg A)$$
$$= P(A)^* P(B \mid A) + P(\neg A)^* P(B \mid \neg A)$$
$$= \alpha^* P(B \mid A) + (1 - \alpha)^* P(B \mid \neg A)$$

for $\alpha = P(A)$. Again, $P(B)$ will be in between $P(B \mid A)$ and $P(B \mid \neg A)$, where all three numbers will be equal precisely when A and B are independent events.

Conditional probabilities and independence are also defined for more than two events. We can condition on several events, and ask what the probability of event A is given that B, C, and D have occurred, and so forth. When we say that several events are independent, we mean that whatever we know about any subset of them does not change the probabilities we assign to the rest. (This is a more demanding requirement than to simply say that any two are independent.)

Random variables are variables that are not up to us to determine (as opposed to decision variables). We can model them as functions over the state space, where each state of nature determines a unique value for the variable, and any uncertainty is encapsulated in the question of which state obtains. For example, assume that I bet with my friend on the roll of a die. I will gain \$1 if it comes up 5, 6, lose \$1 if it comes up 1, 2, and the bet is off if the die falls on 3 or 4. You can think of my net gain as a random variable, X, defined on the states as shown in Table B.1.

Random variables are characterized by their *distributions*, which specify (i) the list of all the values that the random variable might assume; (ii) the probability with which it will assume every such value. In our example, if each state has probability 1/6, the random variable X will assume the value −1 with probability 1/3 (if the state is s_1 or s_2), the value 0 with probability 1/3 (in states s_3 and s_4), and the value 1 also with probability 1/3 (in states s_5 and s_6). Hence the distribution of X can be given as shown in Table B.2.

Table B.1 State and value of X.

State	Value of X
s_1	−1
s_2	−1
s_3	0
s_4	0
s_5	+1
s_6	+1

Table B.2 Value of X and its probability.

Value of X	Its probability
−1	1/3
0	1/3
+1	1/3

When we are interested in the relationship between two random variables, we may analyze their *joint distribution.* Just as the distribution of a single random variable tells us what values it may assume, and with what probabilities, the joint distribution tells us what values each of the variables may assume, and what is the probability that they will assume certain values *simultaneously.* For example, suppose that X measures years of education, and can take the values 10 and 15, whereas Y measures annual income in thousands of dollars, and can take the values 40 and 60. We can draw a table in which every row corresponds to a value of X and every column to a value of Y. In each entry, the joint distribution has the probability that X will take the row value *and* Y will take the column value. Thus, when we sum up *all* numbers in the table we should get 1 (Table B.3).

If we have the joint distribution of two random variables, we can find out the distribution of each of them simply by summation of the numbers in each row (for X) or the numbers in each column (for Y)

Table B.3   Values of X and Y.

	Value of Y	
Value of X	40	60
10	0.4	0.2
15	0.1	0.3

Table B.4   Distributions of X and Y, phase 1.

	Value of Y		
Value of X	20	25	Distribution of X
10	0.4	0.2	0.6
15	0.1	0.3	0.4
Distribution of Y	0.5	0.5	1

(Table B.4). In this context, the distribution of X and the distribution of Y are called the *marginal* distributions, because they can be found at the margins of the joint distribution table.

Two random variables are *independent* if nothing we know about one of them tells us anything new about the other. We have already defined independence of events, but not of random variables. However, this is not supposed to be confusing: the independence of random variables is an extension of the same concept; it states that any event that is defined in terms of one random variable is independent of any event defined in terms of the other. Two random variables are independent if and only if their joint distribution is the product of the marginal distributions (in each and every entry). Clearly, the joint distribution above does not satisfy this condition. There is a unique joint distribution that would make X and Y independent with the same marginal distributions, and it is obtained by taking the product of the relevant marginal distribution values at each entry (Table B.5).

A collection of random variables are independent if nothing we know about any subset of them changes our beliefs about (conditional

Table B.5 Distributions of X and Y, phase 2.

Value of X	Value of Y		Distribution of X
	20	25	
10	0.3	0.3	0.6
15	0.2	0.2	0.4
Distribution of Y	0.5	0.5	1

distributions of) the rest. We have a particular interest in random variables that are independent and also have the same distribution. We call them *i.i.d.* for *identically and independently distributed*.

A numerical random variable such as X has an *expectation* which is a weighted average of its values, where we use the probabilities for the weights. In our case, the expectation of X is

$$E(X) = \mu_X = 1/3 * (-1) + 1/3 * (0) + 1/3 * (+1) = 0$$

As explained in the text, the expectation is very significant in the case of many independent repetitions of the same random variable, because, due to the law of large numbers, with such repetitions we can be quite certain that the average of the random variables will be very close to the expectation. However, in one-shot situations the expectation is but one number that attempts to summarize the information given in the distribution of the random variable, and it is not the only thing that would matter to you.

We are often interested in the degree to which a random variable is dispersed around its expectation. In the context of a monetary asset, this dispersion is associated with the riskiness of the asset. The most popular measures of dispersion are the *variance* and the *standard deviation*. The variance is defined as the expectation of the squared deviation:

$$\text{Var}(X) = E\left[(X - \mu_X)^2\right]$$

and the standard deviation σ_X is the square root of the variance.

The *Normal* distribution is a family of distributions, parameterized by the expectation μ and the standard deviation σ. This family plays a very important role in statistics, due to the *central limit theorem*, which says that, if we look at the average of n i.i.d. random variables (under some additional mild conditions), this average will have a distribution that starts to resemble a Normal distribution more, as n grows to infinity. The law of large numbers has already told us that this average will be close to the expectation μ, but it does not say what the distribution of the average is. With the help of the central limit theorem one can quantify how close is the average to the expectation, without knowing the precise shape of the original distribution.

Solutions

Solutions to odd-numbered exercises are given below.

Chapter 2

1. Flight accidents are typically much more visible than motor
   vehicle accidents. By availability heuristic, we should expect
   that they would be over-represented in our memory, and result
   in an overestimate of the danger of flying. On the other hand,
   the mere numbers of fatalities caused by each mode of transportation aren't the relevant statistics either, because we would
   want to look at these numbers relative to the number of miles
   driven/flown, or to consider some other measures that would
   make it more related to the conditional probability that we face
   in either mode of transportation.
3. One reason may be sheer forgetfulness: once the initial period is
   up, you may simply forget to cancel the subscription, even if at
   first you thought you would. If you planned to cancel the subscription but didn't, this may be a form of dynamic inconsistency. The other obvious reason has to do with habit formation,

---

Making Better Decisions, by Itzhak Gilboa © 2011 John Wiley & Sons, Inc.

the endowment effect, or the status quo bias: before having the magazine you may not value it as much as you would after having consumed it for a while.

5. It stands to reason that this changing the default choice from "opt out" to "opt in" would have a big effect on the number of people choosing to donate organs. One related phenomenon is the anchoring effect: when a decision is the default, it serves as an anchor. It may also be rational to choose it, if you have an implicit belief that the default choice is the norm in the society you live in, and that it probably makes sense if it was chosen to be the norm. Another effect might be simple forgetfulness or unawareness: many people adopt the default choices without ever checking what they are.

Chapter 3

1. The correct answer is (d): this probability cannot be determined without knowing what percentage of overall home owners with a mortgage eventually default.

3. The answer is (d). (a) is true because what we need to compare to make any inference is whether one event (being a journalist) makes the other (being superficial) more likely than it is before knowing anything, and the benchmark of 50% isn't relevant. Clearly, (b) is a point that we made over and over again. Statement (c) is correct, because $P(A \mid B) > P(B \mid A)$ whenever $P(A) > P(B)$.

5. The answer is (c). (a) is false because the probability of A given B is not the same as the probability of B given A. (b) is false because the type of inference we can draw relates the probability of the event to other probabilities of the same events (as in $P(A \mid B) > P(A)$) but not to any specific number such as 50%. Finally, (c) is true, because if the car is not very popular, we may assume that its probability in the entire population is less than 90%, and therefore the probability of finding it in the car repair shop is higher than in the general population. Thus,

$$P(\text{make A}\,|\,\text{problem})=90\% > P(\text{make A})$$

and therefore

$$P(\text{problem}\,|\,\text{make A})> P(\text{problem})$$

and also

$$P(\text{problem}\,|\,\text{make A})> P(\text{problem}\,|\,\text{another make})$$

7. The answer is (a): the Bayesian statistician will indeed have a guess about the unknown parameter even before looking at the sample. But they will take a sample (hence (b) is false). The classical statistician will not generate a confidence interval that they believe is wrong; they will simply avoid stating their beliefs about the specific interval that resulted, saying that they can only quantify beliefs *given* the unknown parameter, and before the sample was taken. Hence (c) is wrong. Finally, (d) is also wrong: classical statistics does not look for counter-intuitive answers, it simply attempts to avoid intuition altogether.

Chapter 4

1. If you assign $u(\$1,000) = 1$ and $u(\$0) = 0$, you find that

$$u(\$700)=0.8 * u(\$1,000)+0.2 * u(\$0)=0.8$$

and then

$$u(\$300)=0.6 * u(\$700)+0.4 * u(\$0)=0.6 * 0.8 = 0.48$$

Thus, the expected utility of lottery A is

$$2/3 * u(\$1,000)+1/3 * u(\$0)=2/3$$

and of lottery B

$$0.5 * u(\$700)+0.5 * u(\$300)=0.5 * 0.8+0.5 * 0.48 = 0.64$$

Since 2/3 > 0.64, you will prefer A to B, and the answer is (a).

3. a. The expected profit is the revenue of $1 minus the expected payoff, which is

$$\$1,000,000 * (1 / 2,400,000) \cong 0.416$$

that is, about 58.4 cents.

b. The statistician is right in observing that the expected profit for each ticket does not change. However, because lottery buyers do not base their decisions solely on their expected gain, the volume of sales might well change as a result of the new policy. Even if a potential lottery buyer were an expected utility maximizer, as long as their utility function is not linear, two lotteries with the same expected value need not be equally attractive to them. (And we may ignore potential buyers who are expected utility maximizers with linear utility functions because they would not buy lottery tickets anyway.) Moreover, using prospect theory we can expect that the higher award will attract more lottery buyers, but that the difference between the probability of 1/2,400,000 vs. 1/4,800,000 will hardly make a difference. Hence, we should not be surprised if the new award structure does indeed attract more buyers and increases profits.

Chapter 5

1. Question (a) compares

$P(\text{snow})$ to $P(\text{two consecutive Heads}) = 0.25$

Question (b) compares

$P(\text{no precipitation})$ to $P(\text{different than } 7) = 36 / 37$

Let's start with (b): if the answer is that

$P(\text{no precipitation}) > 36 / 37$

then it follows that

$$P(\text{snow}) < 1/37$$

and the only answer for (a) that is consistent with this is that snow is less likely than two consecutive Heads.

If, however, the answer is that no precipitation is less likely than a number different than 7, that is, that

$$P(\text{noprecipitation}) < 36/37$$

then we only know that the probability of precipitation is higher than 1/37, but any answer to (a) is consistent with this statement. It is possible that the probability of snow is as high as 1, but also that it is zero, and the probability of precipitation is borne by rain and hail.

3. The majority of participants in Ellsberg's experiments either prefer to bet on known rather than unknown probabilities, or express indifference between a probability that is known to be 50% and a probability that was determined to be 50% by symmetry (between the Democrat and the Republican). Hence Ann's behavior is different from the majority of the participants', and (a) is false. (b) is also false, because a local equity is akin to the known probability, and, if we can make any inference at all, we will probably assume that Ann prefers the foreign equity to the local one. Thus, (c) is true. Finally, (d) is false because a Bayesian model cannot reflect these beliefs.

Chapter 6

1. a. Standard economic theory would suggest that, since interest rates are positive, the employee can only gain by obtaining more money earlier.
    b. The choice can be explained by at least two phenomena, which may be combined. One is lack of self-discipline,

related to dynamic inconsistency: the employee might plan to save money early on to be used later, but suspects that she won't be able to implement this strategy, and therefore prefers that her employer restrict her choices. The other is that the monetary compensation determines her aspiration level, and maybe also her notion of self-worth. In this case, the employee rightly supposes that it will feel better to be on a rising scale, constantly doing better than her aspirations, rather than vice versa.

3. There seems to be nothing wrong with this solution. In (2) you may have raised several considerations against "artificial happiness". The point of the two problems is that avoiding misery (in 3) may be quite different from seeking happiness (in 2).

Index